GOING TO LAW SCHOOL?

GOING TO LAW SCHOOL?

Everything You Need to Know
to Choose and Pursue
a Degree in Law

Harry Castleman and
Christopher Niewoehner

John Wiley & Sons, Inc.
New York • Chichester • Weinheim• Brisbane • Singapore • Toronto

Copyright © 1997 by Harry Castleman and Christopher Niewoehner

Published by John Wiley & Sons, Inc.

Library of Congress Cataloging-in-Publication Data

Castleman, Harry.
      Going to law school? : everything you need to know to choose and
  pursue a degree in law / Harry Castleman and Christopher Niewoehner.
          p.   cm.
      Includes index.
      ISBN 0-471-14907-1 (paper : acid-free paper)
      1. Law schools—United States—Admission. 2. Law—Study and
  teaching—United States. 3. Law—Vocational guidance—United
  States. I. Niewoehner, Christopher, 1970–   . II. Title.
    KF285.C37   1997
    340'.071'173—dc21
                                                            96-51993
                                                            CIP

Printed in the United States of America
10   9   8   7   6   5   4   3   2   1

To our parents,
who helped foot the bill
through law school

CONTENTS

PART TWO
PREPARING FOR LAW SCHOOL

PART THREE
APPLYING AND DECIDING

15 THE ENDGAME 180

ACKNOWLEDGMENTS

Harry would like to thank the following for their help:

First and foremost, Barbara Brown, for graciously slogging through the text on short notice, providing much-needed editing comments, and putting up with an often grumpy and tired co-author.

PJ Dempsey, for nagging a veteran to get back in the game one more time and for believing in a fresh rookie.

Gregg Beloff, Andy Branz, Karen Hurvitz, Ken Ingber, Ken Kurnos, Leslie Lockard, and Megan Wynne, for taking time out of their busy days to try to remember their lives before law school.

Chris would like to thank the following for their help:

Most of all, my parents, for their love, support, and editorial acumen. They have given me all I could ever ask.

There are many others who deserve my heartfelt thanks as well. Elizabeth's experience with law school shaped my approach. Jeanne Hanson provided the initial spark for the book and good advice throughout the project. Malcolm Eaton, Peter Fiutak, Kathryn Kobussen, and Amir Kader provided constant encouragement and generous work space. Finally, Joel Hammerman, Anthony Falzone, Michael Castellano, Rachel Blum, and the entire Great Danes organization shared their application experiences and made me glad to be at law school.

INTRODUCTION

Images of lawyers abound in modern American society. No longer are these dominated by mythical legal wizards like the impossibly perfect Perry Mason, or elegantly tailored barristers like those in *LA Law*, or the shady but sexy practitioners found in a John Grisham novel. Thanks to the relatively recent innovation of allowing cameras in the courtroom, real-life legal maneuvering has become a daily staple on television. Well-publicized trials, such as those of the Menendez brothers and O. J. Simpson, capture our attention for months on end.

Even in our private lives, lawyers seem to be everywhere. Because of the increasingly litigious nature of American society, ordinary citizens personally interact with lawyers in more and more facets of life. This interaction may be as simple as when buying a house or setting up a small business, or more complicated as when going to court to redress an alleged injustice.

Either the cause or the effect (or both) of this increased contact with lawyers is that there are more lawyers in the United States than ever before. There is little likelihood that this trend will decline any time soon. These days, when contemplating a career path, more and more Americans, both of college age and older, are considering attending law school. For some, the process of going to law school and becoming a lawyer is as simple as following in the footsteps of a father, mother, brother, or sister. For most, however, becoming a lawyer is a generalized desire that frequently is not based on much hard information. The entire process seems confusing and convoluted, filled with unknown dangers and procedures that seem designed to trap the unwary.

Going to Law School? will help prospective law students (of whatever age) sort through the issues and concerns that they are (or should be) thinking about. It serves as a guidebook for the traveler making the first tentative steps on the long journey into the legal profession.

Our book is divided into three parts, beginning with seven chapters about choosing law as a career. In the first chapter, we address the most

basic of questions (whether you *want* to become a lawyer) that you
need to answer before beginning the law school application process. In
Chapters 2–5, we explain how law school works and walk you through
the three-year law school process. Part One concludes with two chapters that discuss various types of legal jobs and explain what lawyers
actually do.

We move on to the topic of preparing for law school in Part Two,
covering the time period *before* the application process starts. We suggest things a student can do as an undergraduate that may prove helpful
both in getting into law school and in practicing law. In addition, we
discuss whether it is better for an undergraduate considering law school
to go on to law school right away or to take a break from formal education for a while.

In Part Three, we take you through the entire law school application process. Chapters 10, 11, and 12 review three essential questions
facing anyone considering law school: Which law schools are best for
you? Which law schools might accept you? Which law schools can you
afford? Next, in Chapter 13, we cover a very important part of the law
school application process—the LSAT, the law board tests, which will
have great impact in determining where, if anywhere, your legal education will take place. We explain how the test works and what you can do
to prepare for it. Chapter 14 provides a thorough explanation of how to
complete a law school application and what types of information and
backup materials you will be required to provide. In Chapter 15, we explain the options available after you are either accepted or rejected.

This book—in fact, any one book—cannot answer all the questions
that will arise during the law school application process. Our goal is
simply to provide enough information to answer some of the vital questions and enough guidance to allow you, the prospective law student, to
understand what you are getting into and to realize *what else* you need
to consider before making one of the most important decisions of your
professional life.

GOING TO LAW SCHOOL?

PART ONE

CHOOSING LAW AS A CAREER

1

DO YOU *WANT* TO BE A LAWYER?

The very fact that you are reading this book indicates that you are entertaining the idea of going to law school. We will explain all the nuts and bolts of *how* you can go about accomplishing that goal. However, before we begin explaining all the nuances of preparation courses, the wonders of the LSAT, and the maze of law school applications, we want to reveal a hidden truth to gloss over when thinking about law school: *If you go to law school, you will probably become a lawyer!*

It may sound silly to spell this out, but the point is that it is often too easy, especially for students finishing their undergraduate career, to think about going to law school as an end in itself. One of our goals is to make sure you consider separately two main questions about going to law school. First, do you really want to go to law school and become a lawyer? Only if you can honestly answer "Yes" (or at least "I think so"), should you move on to the second question of how to go about getting into law school.

To decide whether to go to law school and become a lawyer, you need to understand what being a lawyer really means. This involves understanding how law school works (Chapters 2–5), what lawyers actually do (Chapters 6–7), and what qualities are characteristic of and helpful for being a good lawyer.

WHY GO TO LAW SCHOOL?

Lawyers face constant time pressures, ever-expanding work demands, and clients and opponents who are often angry or frustrated. As a result,

3

many lawyers report that they do not really enjoy their profession. Those planning to enter law school should realize this from the outset. Law is a frustrating, highly demanding profession, and the headaches never seem to end. Still, large numbers of people keep marching into law schools, in hopes of joining the ranks. Why?

Some people go to law school because they simply are interested in learning about the rules that govern our society, and they see law school as a continuation of their college education. Some prospective law students are filled with idealism and want to see to it that "justice" prevails. The reality for most law students is that law school is a trade school. It prepares you for a profession, and most people in law school have reached the conclusion that law is the career they wish to pursue.

Too often, college students, after reaching the end of a long academic career, face the daunting problem of finally having to decide what to do with themselves. Deciding to go to law school is an easy fall-back position. It sounds respectable, it impresses family and friends, and it can postpone actually getting a job for another three years! This is probably the worst reason to go to law school. It takes too much time and costs too much money to do it just because there is nothing else around. For these people, going to law school may mean winding up with a law degree and no real idea of what to do with it. Most people go to law school in their twenties, and those years are far too valuable to waste by doing something that will not serve as an important basis for your professional life.

Many people think law is an easy way to get rich. This is also a terrible reason to go to law school. Don't be fooled by the gilt-edged image of lawyers in the media. There are far more lawyers out there making average white-collar salaries than you think. While it is true that you can make a decent living as a lawyer, it is by no means guaranteed that you can move into the world of the fabulously wealthy. For one thing, many lawyers do not wind up in private law practice, and it is only in the upper reaches of private practice that lawyers earn serious money. If you *really* want to make a lot of money, the best advice is to go to business school, where the sky is the limit.

Many lawyers enter the profession because they truly want to help other people. They may lack the manual dexterity to accomplish that goal by building beautiful homes, or they may lack the stomach to operate on sick people, but lawyers in their own way expend their energy trying to help people accomplish their dreams. They may do this by assisting people to buy a new home or set up a new business. They may also help minimize or avoid the bad consequences of an accident or an investment with a con artist. The modern world is a very complicated place, and in any setting those who do not know the inner workings of a system are easily sidetracked or bowled over by someone else who knows the ropes better. Lawyers are experts at navigating the confusing currents of day-to-day living. They help people by providing knowledge of how to get from point A to point B in a way that will, hopefully, be legal and enforceable. Perhaps in an ideal world we would not need lawyers to help guide us in so many areas, but until we reach that state, a good lawyer can provide a lot of help when it is most needed.

So, what *is* a good reason to decide to go to law school? Naturally, that can vary from person to person. One way to try to answer that question is to analyze your personality to see if you have personal skills and characteristics shared by many lawyers (such as being analytical and persistent, with the ability to adapt to different types of people). If you do, and you want to learn more about how the world works, and you love to learn but are not sure how to adapt that learning to a useful trade, then being a lawyer might be a reasonable, logical answer to the old question of "What do you want to be when you grow up?"

LAWYERS' PERSONAL QUALITIES

Along with analyzing why you may want to go to law school, you also need to consider the qualities, both personal and professional, that most lawyers possess. In this way, you can better determine whether you belong among them.

Not everyone has the personality to become a lawyer. That is good, because otherwise everyone would want to go to law school and our society would be even more litigious than it is. The traits that make a good lawyer do not necessarily make a good friend or a good companion. That is one of the reasons why it is so easy to poke fun at lawyers. In popular jokes, lawyers tend to be:

- picky
- two-faced
- argumentative
- evasive
- anxious to exploit an opponent's weakness
- always searching for a loophole

Well, a good lawyer often needs to be *all* of that, and more. That just comes with the territory.

Pickiness/Analytical Nature

If nothing else, lawyers need to be picky. Virtually every task a lawyer works on requires extreme attention to details. For example, in a murder investigation, minute differences in the position and condition of the corpse might prove to be conclusive as to the client's innocence or guilt. In contract negotiations, the exact definition of "net sales" can mean the difference between a healthy profit for the client and a deal where the client is taken to the cleaners by the other side. The only way a lawyer can operate is to become immersed in the details of the case. Because they know how vital details are, lawyers will delve into (almost revel in) the minutiae of a matter. This often exasperates the client, who like most nonlawyers usually focuses on the big picture and the end result.

Of course, experienced lawyers will tame this love affair with the picayune. They learn to adapt it to the real world so that they can differentiate between truly significant details and background facts. However, law students, not yet adept at applying legal analysis to practical problems, can often work themselves up into a fine lather over the most arcane aspects of legal theories. In medieval times, people with this sort of temperament devoted their energies to analyzing esoteric conundrums such as how many angels can dance on the head of a pin. Now, this sort of person winds up in law school, haggling about how to apply obscure court rules of procedure.

The lesson here is that law is based on attention to detail, and it helps immeasurably to be detail-oriented if you want to become a lawyer. If dealing with picky, overanalytical people bothers you, you are in for a lot of irritation practicing as a lawyer.

The flip side of pickiness is an analytical nature, the ability to see beyond the trappings of a situation to the central issues involved. Much of a lawyer's time (and a great deal of a student's time in law school) is spent reviewing a fact pattern and trying to determine the real issues involved. Legal analysis, in theory, is designed to get past the surface trappings and distractions and to focus on the core conflict. For example, when discussing a company's firing of an employee, a lawyer will not focus much attention on the rumors of downsizing that may have swept the office or the brusque manner used to deliver the bad news. Instead, the lawyer wants more information on the wording of the fired worker's employment contract and details on the company's employment practices. These facts are the key to determining if the fired worker has a legitimate claim against the company.

The ability to separate the wheat from the chaff when reviewing a case is one of a lawyer's most valuable tools. It develops, through experience, into the ability to foresee problems and provide protection to a client *before* a problem develops.

Two-Faced/Ability to See Both Sides

The ability to argue both sides of an issue is another skill vital to a lawyer. Outsiders might view this as simply another example of lawyers' lack of ethics or of their "two-faced" nature. A nonlawyer may overlook the fact that arguing a matter from the other side is the best way to see weaknesses in your own arguments, thus helping you do a better job of presenting your point of view. Lawyers often find themselves arguing for two different clients, each with diametrically opposed interests. Naturally, some lawyers specialize in certain areas. It is not uncommon for one lawyer to become known as a "tenant's lawyer," while another is a "landlord's lawyer." A lawyer may make a career of advocating only one particular point of view, such as increased rights for a specific group or the defense of accused criminals. Still, in essence, most lawyers are often just hired guns, retained advocates who do not necessarily espouse their own personal ideas or beliefs. A lawyer's job is to make the client's position appear more logical, more appealing, and more in line with the existing laws than the other side's, and so help the client to prevail. Therefore, a person who can only advocate ideas he or she personally believes in will be severely limited as a lawyer. It takes only a modicum of talent to try to convince people of ideas you believe in. It takes much more talent to be convincing on behalf of somebody else's (possibly unsympathetic) ideas.

Argumentative Nature

Being argumentative is a specialty of those lawyers who specialize in litigation (i.e., those who try cases and appear regularly in court). Litigation is, after all, the art of conducting a "battle" between opposing sides, and it brings out the argumentative personality. To be argumentative in a litigation situation just means that you are forcefully advocating your client's position. You need to be persuasive in your court presentation, as simple bluster and bravado will not often suffice. In arguing court cases, it helps if you love the parry and thrust of verbal combat. Nonlitigation situations often call for just the opposite, a more conciliatory person willing to compromise.

Evasiveness/Caution

Lawyers may often appear to be evasive, in that they hedge their bets and do not answer questions fully and directly. Part of this, like many attributes a lawyer presents to the world, is a negotiation technique. In any interaction, a lawyer will not want to promise more than the client is willing to agree to, and a lawyer may wish to avoid conceding a point now when it can be traded later for some concession by the other side.

The complexity and difficulty of many laws often makes it difficult to predict with absolute certainty the outcome of any legal squabble. Thus, lawyers are often forced to be somewhat evasive even with their own clients. The client might prefer the lawyer to say, "Oh, no question, you'll win this case!" The truth is that lawyers know all too well that the outcome can hinge on personalities and fact nuances beyond their control. Lawyers are thus reluctant to go too far out on a limb on almost anything. They feel much safer basing their statements on verifiable, concrete facts. A lawyer will be happy to tell you that the client signing a new acquisition agreement is a corporation established in this or that state, and that the corporation properly approved the signing of the agreement. A lawyer will, however, try hard to avoid saying that the agreement complies with all laws or that, when the deal closes, the assets bought will be owned free and clear of any possible conflicting ownership claims. For these less clear-cut questions, the lawyer will embellish the answer with caveats and exceptions.

This reluctance to make broad general statements is annoying but necessary. Lawyers know how to turn seemingly absolute certainties upside down, so that the extremely unlikely is treated as very probable. Lawyers are trained not to assume anything. A perfect example of this is a lesson Harry remembers best from his law school class on wills. The professor loved to explain that long before the days when medicine allowed women of older ages to bear children, lawyers who drafted wills were trained *never* to rule out the possibility that an elderly woman (even one over eighty) might have another child and thus change the distribution of her assets after death. The class always laughed at this story, but the lesson was clear: having a naturally cautious personality is a plus for a lawyer. Lawyers do not gain much advantage by jumping to conclusions. In fact, just the opposite is true.

Ability to Exploit an Opponent's Weakness

If you say that lawyers exploit the weakness of opponents, most straightforward lawyers will wonder why you find that disturbing. After all, the lawyer will say, why did the client hire me to begin with? Nine times out of ten it is to help the client get maximum advantage from a situation. Recognizing, identifying, and using the other side's weakness is often the lawyer's most effective way to advance the client's cause.

A Love of Loopholes

The lawyer's love of loopholes springs from the same source. Clients hire lawyers to find and use loopholes. A lawyer who ignores loopholes (or at least fails to mention them to a client) is not only doing a bad job but is liable to a claim for malpractice from an angry client.

Special Skills Needed In Court

While the six preceding traits are, in general, found among lawyers as a group, certain types of lawyers tend to emphasize some traits over others. As we discuss in Chapter 7, there are many different types of lawyers, who perform very different types of tasks. Litigators, the most famous type, appear in court and orchestrate trials. They need special skills that are less important in the nonlitigation world (where it is harder to pigeonhole legal personalities). Litigators tend to fall into one of two types: the actor and the athlete.

The Actor

Theatrical lawyers love the drama and suspense of a courtroom setting. They relish the role of leading man or lady, with the judge and jury as the "audience" waiting on their every word. Courtroom performance requires a keen sense of timing and a flair for dramatic effect. You must know when to hold back and when to spring forth, firing a devastating salvo at the opposition. After the trial, waiting for the decision from judge or jury is like waiting for the reviews after a play's opening night.

The Athlete

The other main type of litigator is the athlete (usually the *frustrated* athlete, when it comes to lawyers), who views the trial as another form of sports competition. It is always "us" versus "them" to these lawyers, and it is easy for the competitive sort to work themselves into an agitated state over an ongoing case. They become very emotionally involved in the proceedings and will try to use the force of their personality to push their way to victory. They are used to the drill of combat. You train, you work together, you go head-to-head with the other side, and you see who wins.

Despite the high-profile nature of some legal tasks, such as "performing" in the courtroom, we want to emphasize that lawyers rarely take the decisive role in a case. A trial lawyer appears to be the central figure in the courtroom drama, but the truth is that the trial lawyer is only dealing with a situation established by others. Similarly, a clever barrister can manipulate a business situation only to a certain degree, by use of skill and "tricks of the trade" picked up over the years. Orchestrating a billion-dollar corporate takeover, the lawyer cannot make the basic business decisions that drive or sink a deal. Lawyers are, in essence, secondary characters who must cater to the whims and desires of clients who have their own agendas. If what you really want is to control your professional playing field, find another career. Law will frustrate you and leave you yearning for more open spaces.

The Need to Relate Well with People

Most of the personal qualities mentioned so far come from a person's inner mental workings. This is because, at heart, law is a very mental sort of world. Most of a lawyer's work is done behind the scenes: reviewing documents, studying statutes, and analyzing cases. As a result, law schools are often filled with brainy kids who are underdeveloped in the social skills area (we each must plead guilty to this charge). Most law students may not be as "nerdy" as some who go into computer programming or engineering, but law schools are rarely filled with former winners of the Mister or Miss Congeniality award. Mental ability alone, however, will not be enough to be a successful lawyer. A good lawyer has to develop the ability to handle people as well. It's all well and good to understand all the laws and cases concerning divorce and child custody. If you cannot relate to and understand the emotions of the living, breathing people who walk into your office, you will never be able to adequately represent your clients.

For that matter, if you have problems relating to people, you will find it very difficult to *get* clients. Getting out of school and joining the real world presents a rude awakening to many students. One of the harshest lessons new lawyers in private practice learn is that the ability to attract and keep a steady stream of clients is the most valuable trait a lawyer in that situation can possess. A lawyer who can combine the intellectual ability to see the legal issues involved in a dispute with the personal magnetism to inspire confidence and attract clients will have few problems moving up in the legal profession. Unfortunately, most people find it very difficult to combine these two traits.

LAWYERS' PROFESSIONAL TRAITS

There are other aspects of a lawyer's nature that tend to be called forth by the nature of the legal profession. The most important of these professional traits are:

- commitment to your career
- a serious attitude
- an ethical nature

Career Commitment

Working in the legal field requires concerted, steady effort because of the economics and work habits of the law business. Most legal jobs (especially those in private practice) require great commitments of time and effort in order to prove profitable. Attorneys tend to be very busy, with a million things going on at once, and they are always at their clients' beck and call. Clients call up at inopportune moments with problems that just can't wait. A long-planned vacation may need to be canceled when, at the last minute, some settlement you have been working on reaches a roadblock and you need to stay to see it through. Of course, many professionals have similar problems, but lawyers tend to have more than most.

Harry recalls a classic case when another lawyer in his office literally stood up and walked out in the middle of an all-day negotiating session because he was to be married in a few hours and had to leave to catch a plane. Harry was the "lucky" one who took his place at the table and had to work through the entire Labor Day weekend on a deal that simply *had* to close before the next business day.

Being a lawyer does not always involve such extreme time demands, but because of the intense attention the job often requires, many lawyers frankly find it difficult to maintain a normal home life. Hours are long, and work frequently interrupts family time. It is for these reasons that old-time lawyers will wink at young recruits and warn that "the law is a jealous mistress."

Seriousness

Lawyers also must develop a serious attitude. While the days have long since passed when the image of the average lawyer was that of a dour sourpuss with a drab personality, very few modern lawyers are flashy and glib. This may stem from the fact that lawyers come from a set of students who never were social superstars, but it also relates to the nature of lawyers' work. They often deal with issues that are very important to clients, and lightheartedness and jocularity are usually inappropriate. When clients are explaining to you how they were horribly disfigured in an industrial accident, or that they are worried that the scheduled purchase of their "dream home" is about to fall apart, they will not be too interested in hearing some smart-aleck one-liner from you. When you deal with serious issues, people expect you to act accordingly.

For example, at many firms it is common for lawyers or staff members to surreptitiously make sure no clients are present before regaling the office with some raucous or ribald story.

Ethical Nature

Despite the current trend of lawyer-bashing, it must be emphasized that lawyers need to be, and usually are, highly ethical. Counseling clients will allow you to learn more about them than you may really wish to know. Under the fairly rigid rules of professional ethics that govern lawyers, you must keep most of that information confidential. These rules also prevent lawyers from taking cases involving conflicts of interest with other clients and govern the way clients' funds are handled. Lawyers risk serious professional punishment for straying in this area.

On the surface, the tasks performed by lawyers representing a business in contract negotiations are very similar to those of any business negotiator who is attempting to arrange the most favorable deal for the company. However, of the two, it is only the lawyer who is bound by rules of professional ethics. The crafty lawyer may bend and stretch these rules, but if the rules are broken, the lawyer risks professional censure and even loss of the ability to practice. Business negotiators are not bound by any rules. Thus, one could say that people should trust lawyers more than the layperson, but it rarely works out that way. The general public distrusts the fact that lawyers are "hired guns," willing to work for any client who comes along. The average citizen dislikes the fact that hiring a lawyer is now often a necessity, even for ordinary transactions.

It may sound quaint, but lawyers are simply not permitted to lie. They can be very adept at allowing carefully chosen words to give a misleading impression, and they can be masters at avoiding a direct response, but under their professional code lawyers may not flat-out lie. Few other professions place such high value on truthfulness, and that is why a lawyer will usually rely on the word of another lawyer, even if the latter is on the "other side." Of course, many nonlawyers do not appreciate how devious lawyers can be when trying to avoid out-and-out lies. Unlike fellow lawyers, who know all too well how lawyers can twist words into unrecognizable lumps, lay people are often misled by the seemingly authoritative pronouncements from lawyers' lips. They then feel particularly resentful when they learn that there was a "catch" to what the lawyer said. For example, a lawyer could, without batting an eye, confidently state that client X has only $30,000 to his name in the whole wide world. What remains unsaid is that five minutes ago client X transferred $7 million to a revocable trust or to a shell corporation set up in the Cayman Islands or some other equally remote outpost the opposing side is unlikely to discover. Some call that lying. Lawyers call it advancing a client's cause. The lesson here is to try to read behind anything someone else's lawyer tells you, and try as much as possible to get direct answers from a lawyer. Good luck.

IS GOING TO LAW SCHOOL WORTH THE COST?

In addition to comparing your personal skills and characteristics against those of most lawyers, you should undertake a serious cost-benefit analysis of the issue of whether to go to law school. To do this, you must balance what you will be giving up in order to earn a law degree against what you will gain.

The Expense of Law School

First of all, going to law school is expensive. Be forewarned that, throughout this book, we will return to the topic of money and how much law school costs. That's because it costs *a lot*. Tuition at a private law school can easily top $20,000 per year, not including room and board or other living expenses. Triple this to see how much three years of law school will set you back. Where is that money going to come from? We examine the specifics of law school finances in more detail in Chapter 12, but at this point we just review the highlights.

As with undergraduate college, there are three primary sources of funds for law school:

- parents
- savings
- loans

No matter which combination of these sources you choose, going to law school is a serious commitment of resources you should not enter into lightly.

Financial Support from Parents

This is all well and good, if you are lucky enough to have that much family cash available. Still, money your parents spend on your law school expenses might otherwise have gone toward a down payment for your first house, starting your own business enterprise, or your future savings.

Savings from Your Own Work

Truly, this is the most admirable source of support. It is always a matter of pride to say, years later, "I earned all my law school tuition *myself.*" Again, though, using your hard-earned savings on three years of expensive tuition means those funds will not be available for other needs that might later develop. There are few things harder for a young adult to do than to begin a serious savings plan for future needs. Depleting what resources you have for law school will leave you without much of a financial cushion (if you have a cushion at all at this point in your life). Trying to earn enough money during law school to pay a significant portion of your tuition expenses is theoretically possible. In practice, however, doing so will seriously drain your time and energy, risking your ability to perform up to your potential in class.

Student Loans

If you can qualify, loans designed especially for students, at government-supported low interest rates, are a great way to avoid shelling out cash up front for law school. The problem with these loans is that, even at artificially low interest rates, three years of loans still add up to a considerable debt obligation after graduation. Most of these loan plans offer a waiting period after graduation (usually a year or so), during which you do not need to start repayments. This way, the ex-student has some time to get a job and begin earning a salary before starting to repay the debt.

A delay in beginning loan repayments sounds great to the novice student just beginning the law school process, who is dreaming of the huge salaries paid to new lawyers by top big-city firms. Well, if you are one of the fortunate few who "hit the jackpot" and hook up with a mega-firm after graduation, repaying student loans at minimal interest rates will not hurt that much, and your financial gamble will have paid off. However, very few law students obtain those high-salary slots. Many law school graduates wind up, a year after the end of school, working for only moderate salaries at medium or small firms or in government positions. Many others may not find law jobs at all. The repayment deferral period on student loans can slip by quickly, and suddenly these graduates must face the cold reality of dealing with a significant loan payment each month. For almost any young graduate, siphoning off a regular portion of income soon after entering the job market will cause financial pressures. This problem is compounded if the graduate is starting a new family at the same time and dealing with the extra money demands that causes.

The point of this financial lecture is that no matter how you finance it, law school will likely cause some form of monetary strain. This may range from the bothersome to the downright draining, and you should only undertake the process if you really think it is the best thing for you to do. These days, for a large segment of American society, undergraduate college (which can also cost a lot of money) is basically a requirement for future professional success. Law school, however, is not the same. You do not need to go to law school. There are lots of other things you can do with three years of your life.

IS THIS WHAT YOU WANT TO DO FOR THREE YEARS?

It's not just the money either. If you are smart or resourceful (and most people who wind up in law school are), you will probably find some way to earn a decent living and be able to pay off your loans or replenish the money used for law school. More important is the fact that for most people, law school comes at a prime period of life (the time between twenty and thirty years of age). In many ways, this decade is the most significant in a person's life. The friends and acquaintances you meet, and the personal and professional choices you make, during this period will mold a good chunk of your entire life. As a rule, people have more intellectual growth and creative drive during this period than at any other time. If you "waste" a third of your twenties going to law school, you have squandered a precious resource no future financial windfall can replenish.

Getting through three years of law school may expand your knowledge and develop your analytical thinking, but that may not do you much good if in the end you decide you do not want to go into law or if you find that you cannot get the kind of job you want. At that point, it will be even harder to devote another chunk of money and time to begin pursuing another career goal. You can never get back those three years when you could have pursued other interests. The old maxim "time waits for no one" is a cliché, but it is still true. You only get so many shots at starting out.

Naturally, when you consider whether to go to law school, you can never be *certain* that it is the right thing for you. Only the superorganized decide on law careers back in junior high and stick to the decision to the end. All you can do when contemplating a law career is to take a realistic look at yourself, analyze your various traits, and compare them to the traits lawyers need. You also need to clearly understand what it will take to get through the law school application process and the three years of law school that follow and, beyond that, what it really means to be a lawyer. If this book does nothing else, it should warn you *not* to go to law school just because you can't think of anything better to do after college or because your family told you for years that you should, or because some of your friends plan on going.

Both of us were smart enough (or lucky enough) to resist the herd mentality of going on to law school right after college. In fact, we both decided during our senior year of college that we did *not* want to become lawyers. In both our cases, it was only after college, when we were directly exposed to lawyers and law students who could explain and vouch for how the law school process really worked, that we each decided to take the plunge.

You should decide to go to law school (if, in fact, you decide to go) because, in your best judgment, a law career is right for your talents and temperament, and working in law seems like something you want to do for an appreciable part of your professional life. We cannot tell you if law school is right for you. What we can do is give you information to help you make an educated decision. If, years later, you decide in retrospect that you chose correctly, you can, of course, credit your clear thinking and good judgment. If, on the other hand, you decide you made the wrong choice, you will at least have the comfort of knowing that you gave it serious thought and didn't jump into it blindly.

2

HOW LAW
SCHOOL WORKS

So far, this book has discussed the big picture. What do you want to be when you grow up? Do you really *want* to be a lawyer? Now it's time to ease up a bit and start looking at some more practical issues. Before you firmly decide on law, you should understand how law school actually works, as this is the first stage in a legal career.

THE SOCRATIC METHOD
OF TEACHING

The primary thing to understand about law school is that it is very different from most undergraduate colleges. You probably already assume that law courses will not resemble those you took in college, and you are correct. What may come as a surprise is that the very nature of the teaching at law school is different from what you are used to. Law professors generally use the "Socratic method" (or, in less grandiose terminology, the "case method") of teaching, and this will require some adjustment in how you approach your classes.

In traditional undergraduate education, students read a textbook that reviews and summarizes the topic under scrutiny. In class, the professor spends most of the hour lecturing on the topics covered in the text, helping to explain and elucidate the points covered. Students are, of course, called on occasionally to answer or explain particular points. However, the process largely consists of the professor spewing forth information, which the students are expected to regurgitate during exams.

19

Tests are largely exercises in proving that you read the material and that you understood the basic precepts discussed in class. The whole thing is largely a one-way street. The professor spells it out for you, and all you have to do is prove you paid attention. Under the Socratic method, things are not so easy.

The Socratic method is named after Socrates, the ancient Greek philosopher. Legend has it that he taught his disciples by forcing them to teach themselves through a process of logically working through issues in their own minds. Socrates accomplished this by serving more as a moderator than a lecturer. He peppered his students with leading questions that required far more thorough understanding of the problems than just filling in the blanks.

Many law professors try to emulate this ideal, especially in classes for first-year law students. The core concept is that students will learn more if they are forced to explain an issue themselves rather than having it all explained to them outright. Guess what? They're right. Instinctively, you probably already know this. If you ask someone a question and receive a simple answer, that resolves your immediate problem. However, you may have missed (or not fully grasped) the reasons *why* the correct answer is right. Until you do that, you will probably be unable to answer the next problem that comes along with slightly different facts. If, however, the person you asked stops and helps you explain *why* the right answer is right, you will probably get more of the big picture. At least, you will feel far more confident that you really understand the answer.

Textbooks

In law school the texts you use will be unlike almost any other school books you have studied. Rather than providing you with general discussions of various legal precepts, the books present excerpts of court decisions, organized by topic. By following several cases revolving around a particular legal theory, you learn how judges handled the issue in varying situations. Sometimes the cases reach different conclusions, because key facts were different and led to different results. The underlying legal concept usually remains uniform. On the other hand, sometimes the cases will reach opposite conclusions, even when they are dealing with virtually identical facts. This tends to occur when the judges ruling on the cases held different beliefs or when the basic legal philosophy changed between the times of the two cases.

Basing legal education on court cases is very appropriate, because law is heavily based on precedents. A judge faced with a legal issue is supposed to decide only on an interpretation of what *existing* law provides. That law may be specific statutes passed by the legislature, or regulations adopted by government agencies. It may also be case law, the law that developed slowly, through decades of judicial decisions, filling the gaps where statutes and regulations did not provide clear-cut guidelines. Similarly, a law student learns how the law handles an issue by studying the rulings of significant or representative cases from the past that addressed that issue.

To prepare for class, the law student who reads case excerpts in the textbook is supposed to summarize, or brief, each case covered in the assigned sections. A brief should include the basic fact pattern, the decision, and most important, the reasoning used by the judge to reach the decision. Briefing helps students think through the problem and summarize the salient facts. Having done this, a student will find it much easier to discuss the case in class if called on.

Class Procedure

In class, professors may provide a short introduction to the day's topic. More likely, however, they may simply look around the room, pick out some student trying to hide behind a notebook, and ask the poor soul to recite the facts of the case in question. A simple recitation of facts will rarely be enough to get the student off the hook. Next come some probing questions about the basis of the decision, followed by difficult questions that involve changing one or two facts from the current case and inquiring whether that would change the outcome. Only after the student has demonstrated an understanding of the core concept by applying it to new situations (or after the student has displayed a clear-cut *lack* of understanding) will the professor move on to new prey.

For students used to the nonthreatening process of simply scribbling down notes while the professor drones on about the day's topic, this Socratic system may come as a rude awakening. It literally turns the spotlight on the students. This aggressive line of questioning from the teacher who could just as easily *tell* you the answer can produce waves of nausea in students afflicted with stage fright. You just never know when the professor will happen to glance your way and redirect the inquisition to *you*.

In the beginning of the first year of law school, this unfamiliar method of teaching can lead to wholesale panic. Some may fall right into the verbal traps set by the professor for the smart-aleck student who thinks the answer is simple. Other students may get flustered and make silly mistakes that result in deep embarrassment in front of their peers. Most students find it impossible to stand up to a professor and challenge the teacher who might be deliberately leading the class down the wrong path, just to see who will be smart (or brave) enough to speak the truth.

We both found the Socratic system to be more frustrating than terrifying. At first, we kept wishing the professor would simply tell us the answer he was trying to drag out of some poor student. Over time, we came to see the value of this teaching method. It forces smart-aleck hotshots who hardly worked up a sweat throughout college (such as yours truly) to realize that in law school you really do have to work much harder to fully learn what is being taught.

Three Rules to Remember

After the initial shock at the new Socratic classroom technique wears off, most attentive law students will adapt their studying methods to fit the new format, and they learn these three essential rules for handling this teaching style:

1. The cardinal rule is, as much as possible *never* fall behind in your reading. It's one thing to fail to grasp properly the legal nuance buried away in some centuries-old case you read. It is quite another to simply be unable to recite the facts of a case when called on because you did not yet read that day's assignment.
2. The second essential rule is, sharpen your summarizing skills. All legal analysis can be boiled down to one phrase: think precisely and ignore the superfluous. Law students must learn to see what is legally important in a situation and what is just window dressing.
3. The final major rule is, always think on your feet. Simply memorizing the facts and decision of a case will not be very helpful when,

thirty seconds into your response, the professor interrupts and throws you a curve ball by completely changing the facts and asking how that would alter the outcome.

Many students find it difficult to adapt to this new method of teaching, especially if they are naturally shy and not prone to public speaking. Still, this baptism by fire at the beginning of law school is ultimately valuable. It forces students to learn to think clearly and to defend their ideas against vigorous challenges. If you cannot learn to do those two things, you will probably not make a very good lawyer, so you might as well find out now. In any event, the Socratic style is not so prevalent in second- and third-year law school classes, and by then most students have come to terms with the method.

Beware of the First Day of Class

Another change from college procedure, which is connected with the Socratic method of teaching, reveals itself at the very start of law school. Students may be used to an easygoing first day of class from their undergraduate days, when the teacher might ramble on for a while about the course topics, assign some light reading, and then dismiss class after only half the period was over. This is not the way law school classes begin. Before you even set foot in your first law school class, your professors will more than likely have posted reading assignments on the notice board. If you come into the first class without having at least read the assignment, you are courting the trauma and humiliation of having your ignorance of the day's topic publicly displayed. The professor will likely surprise you by calling your name for an explanation of some case you have never heard of. The best advice if you make this mistake is, do not let it happen again, because you *will* be called on in the next class or two.

EXAMS AND GRADES

Another major difference between law school and undergraduate college is that in law school your entire grade may depend on how well you do on your final exams. For the most part, there are no papers, no mid-terms, and no pop quizzes. In fact, during the first year, some courses last all year long, so you may spend the entire year without ever taking a test until the dreaded final exam at year's end. This can be extraordinarily nerve-wracking, especially because, during first year, you may feel uncertain about whether you are understanding the topics at all. With no interim tests, you have no real measure to see if you are at least close to where you should be.

Fortunately, some more humane law school professors do schedule "practice" exams halfway through the course. These exams will probably not count toward your final grade, but they will at least give you an idea of where you stand. If you do well, you can feel more confident. If you do poorly, you at least have some time to try to catch up. In addition, some professors give weight to in-class contributions when assigning grades, so the final exam may not be your *only* shot at success.

The final exams are hours-long essay tests. They usually consist of convoluted fact patterns that raise a myriad of legal issues. Your job is to analyze the situations and write out your conclusions. What new law students often find hard to realize is that the main goal in the exams is not necessarily to find the right answers (there may not be any) but to spot the significant legal issues and provide a cogent analysis of those issues.

Let's not mince words. Law school grades are *very* important. With such an overabundance of law students spewing forth from America's law schools, the primary criterion used by employers to judge applicants is their grade-point average. A student at a second-tier law school who comes in near the top of the class will usually have a better chance of landing a good job than a student at a prestigious law school who is in the bottom half of the class.

With grades so important and exams so infrequent, law students face a pressure cooker situation as the school year goes by, and keeping up with the workload becomes harder and harder. Keep in mind that the first year is, after all, only one-third of your law school career. By excelling in the last two years, you can to some extent make up for mediocre grades at the beginning. Still, first-year grades carry a lot of weight. They will heavily influence your first serious law job, the summer clerkship for which you interview in the fall of the second year, when first-year grades are all you have to show your legal prowess. The best advice is to work extra hard during the first year of law school. The first year is unquestionably the hardest, and if you can make it through the first year with good grades, the last two years should be a relative breeze. If you find yourself feeling lost, try to get help right away, either from other students or from the faculty. If you drift and let yourself slip further and further behind, you may finish the first year of law school in a rut that you will not be able to climb out of even over the next two years.

3

FIRST-YEAR COURSES

With so many law schools in the United States, it is impossible to predict exactly which courses all first-year law students will take. But most law schools provide a fairly standard first-year curriculum, consisting of the following basic courses:

- Civil Procedure
- Constitutional Law
- Contracts
- Real Property
- Torts
- Criminal Law
- Legal Research and Writing

There are few, if any, elective courses. These first-year courses cover the basic building blocks of law. In many cases, these courses are not meant to provide practical legal training but rather to introduce students to legal concepts that form the basis of our legal system.

CIVIL PROCEDURE

This course immediately immerses new law students in the arcane minutiae of procedural legal wrangling. Civil Procedure teaches the procedural law, the "inside" rules of court. These apply to civil court cases, which are those brought by one private party against another, as distinguished from criminal cases, where the government charges someone with committing a crime. Most courts in the United States can be cate-

26

gorized as federal courts (those operated by the federal government) or state courts (those operated by the individual states). Civil Procedure classes only cover the rules that apply in the federal court system. The focus on federal rules is deliberate, as federal rules are virtually uniform throughout the country, whereas state rules vary widely from one state to another.

At first, this course may seem impossibly dull. You learn what kind of cases can be brought in federal courts, what sort of information to include when you file a complaint to begin a suit, and how long you have after an incident to file a lawsuit. It also covers an entire laundry list of objections that the defense can raise to try to toss out a lawsuit without ever having a judge rule on the underlying merits of the claim. Then there are all the rules governing the actions of both sides in the time leading up to a trial, a myriad of rules governing the conduct of a trial, and a confusing array of procedures to follow after a trial, when considering an appeal of the verdict. These technical rules seem to confirm all the bad feelings nonlawyers have about the legal profession. They focus excessively on picky details and technicalities without dealing with the "real" question of right or wrong.

After a few months, however, you will begin to appreciate the reasons why all these rules exist. For one thing, the rules that determine which cases can be heard in federal court are designed to keep the case load down. Federal courts would be overwhelmed were it not for the rules requiring certain cases to be heard in state courts. More important, these technical rules often serve as the basic cornerstone of preserving the rights of both plaintiff and defendant. For example, the statute of limitations (which bars a person from suing if he or she waits too long after the incident) preserves the rights of the defendant to avoid being forced to respond to claims concerning events long-forgotten by those involved.

While you will probably come to appreciate this class only once you have begun practicing law, it is unlikely you will find Civil Procedure to be your most scintillating course. Those who intend to avoid litigation and focus on a business or government practice may question the value of learning court rules they may never have cause to use. But all lawyers, even those who never set foot in a courtroom, need to have some basic knowledge of how courts work and how court cases proceed. The Civil Procedure course accomplishes that task. If taught by a bright, lively professor, it can be an eye-opening hands-on introduction to the real world of lawyering. Taught by a tired, unimaginative professor, this course can be a quagmire of endless rules that seem to have no real cohesion.

CONSTITUTIONAL LAW

If Civil Procedure deals with specifics, Constitutional Law is almost all theory with a big dash of history tossed in. Almost like an undergraduate seminar, the constitutional law course breezes through over two hundred years of significant federal court cases. The course covers seminal topics such as the ability of courts to declare laws unconstitutional and the limits of government powers during wartime. It also covers how laws meant to abolish all vestiges of slavery were circumvented to continue discrimination long after the Civil War and how "legal" discrimination was finally abolished. Moving to more recent eras, the course examines how the federal government gained control over many areas that had once been considered beyond its reach, how the doctrine of "one man, one vote" became set in stone, and how "privacy rights" came to be the basis for legalizing abortions.

It is in Constitutional Law (affectionately known as "Con Law") that you will finally discover some of the details behind the famous cases you may have heard about, such as *Marbury vs. Madison, Brown vs. Board of Education,* and *Roe vs. Wade.* Students with a love for history should lap this course up, but even those who are not history junkies need to learn how the courts became the arbiters of the most burning political questions of the past two hundred years. Studying these cases shows how the role of the courts has changed greatly since the adoption of the U.S. Constitution, sheds light on how our present legal and political world evolved, and highlights how some basic conflicts were legally "solved" in very different manners in different eras. Appreciating how courts can sway with the political breeze teaches students a lesson all lawyers must grasp: our laws are always open to new and different interpretations that can drastically change what is considered legal.

CONTRACTS

First-year law students without much business experience may view Contracts class as boring, dull, and slow. While Contracts cases do not deal with big issues of historical importance as do those in Constitutional Law, they can be the most ultimately valuable class taken during the first year in law school. Virtually every business transaction involves a contract, one way or another. When you decide to buy a car, you and the dealer enter into a contract. When you buy a house, you enter into a contract with the seller. When a company hires you as an employee, you have created a contract. When you order some cubic zirconium jewelry over a cable shopping network, you are entering into a contract. When the U.S. government orders twenty F-16 bombers, it too enters into a contract. Big or small, significant or petty, business transactions revolve around the law of contracts. Learning what has to happen before the two sides actually form a contract, what rights you gain by being a party to a contract, and what you can do if the other side breaches a contract term can have real, practical benefits to almost every lawyer.

Contracts class usually begins fairly slowly. Much attention is paid to detailed analyses of when contracts are legally formed. At first blush, that may seem a very simple question ("It's when you *sign* the contract, silly!"). As with most everything in law, things are not quite as simple as they appear. Frequently, you may form a contract without ever signing on the dotted line. The essence of a contract is when one side makes an offer that the other side accepts and the two sides exchange something of value. So, Contracts class begins with trying to decide what is an offer and what is acceptance (rather than just a counteroffer). Then comes trying to pinpoint the exact moment when you have a contract. Once you pass this point, Contracts class gets into meatier discussions of the rules that govern the operation of contracts and how you can read unwritten rules into written contracts. Next comes the more lively topic of what sort of acts will be considered breaches of contracts, and what you can do if the other side defaults. For example, if your department store promises to deliver your new refrigerator on Thursday and doesn't bring it until Friday morning, can you say, "Sorry, you breached our contract, I'm not paying you a dime"? If Continental Can Co. orders

5,000 widgets from Amalgamated Industries, and Amalgamated delivers only 4,987 of them, can Continental Can sue Amalgamated? The answer, of course, is, "It depends. . . ." In Contracts class, at least you will learn what the answers to these questions depend upon.

REAL PROPERTY

If you expect Contracts class to be dry and dusty, just wait until you get to Real Property! Here, for the first half of the course, you'll be lucky to read any cases from the time since your parents were born. Studying two-hundred-year-old cases in Real Property class is not at all unusual. Some cases even go back to the 1300s. The reason for all the antiquity is that the law of land (also known as real estate or real property) has not changed much from the feudal days of medieval England. American law is, after all, based on the old law of England. When it comes to studying the rules that govern the buying, selling, and ownership of land, reviewing a medieval case from across the Atlantic makes perfect sense.

One of the hardest parts of getting into Real Property law is the archaic terms that are used. To truly understand the basics of the various ways you can own rights to real estate, you need to learn the subtle differences between a fee simple and a fee tail. To fully understand the nuances of how title to land passes, you must learn about livery of seisin. Once you graduate from law school, it is unlikely that you will ever use those terms in a meaningful way, but if you can adjust yourself to accept these ancient concepts, you will survive the hardest part of a Real Property course.

Once you make it to the twentieth century, things pick up. You begin to deal with issues you have actually heard about. Topics covered include local zoning laws and how far cities can go in regulating use of property by landowners, the rules covering condominium purchases, and environmental regulations and how they can affect your plans for the land you just bought. Since all these ideas are considered new-fangled in the staid world of real property law, your professor may give them short shrift and try to squeeze them into the last few months of class. These "trendy" topics will give you some sense of how real estate issues are dealt with today rather than in the Mesozoic era, where you may spend most of the year.

TORTS

Torts is a funny name. Few first-year law students have any concrete knowledge of what the name means before they pick up the textbook. To give you a head start, we can let you in on the secret: A tort is a wrong committed by someone who injures another person in some way. If you are the victim of a tort, you may sue the tortfeasor (the one who harmed you) in a court of law. Tort cases are civil cases, that is, they are brought by you individually, not brought by the state because of failure to comply with a specific statute. The types of incidents that constitute torts are endless. Allowing ice to build up in front of your store so that passersby slip and fall, slapping someone in the face, or deliberately scaring someone are all forms of torts. The law, at least theoretically, provides remedies for those who are on the receiving end. Memorable highlights of Torts class will probably be a few nauseating cases involving finding gruesome things in bottles or soda cans, and what you can do to those responsible for allowing the "foreign matter" to wind up in such unlikely places. More practical will be examinations of negligence cases, such as medical malpractice, which encompass a great deal of modern litigation. Even more current is the issue of product liability, which determines who is responsible for injuries caused by defective products. Is it the parts manufacturer who supplied a faulty component? Is it the manufacturer who packaged the unit and sent it into the world of commerce? Is it the local distributor who actually sold the product to you? Or is it the friendly repairman, who failed to detect the defect before it was too late? Extra credit to those who answered, "Sue all of them, and see who has the most insurance."

Allocating risk of injuries from defective products is a hotly debated concept these days, so it will not be hard for students to get worked up over this topic. It is here that Torts class may truly develop your legal thinking. You have to train yourself to examine the facts of a case to logically determine who should be held legally responsible for some harm. It is not enough to just feel sorry for the victims and try to find somebody to reimburse them (although there is a strain of recent cases that seemingly adopt that philosophy). Studying these topics helps develop a dispassionate, orderly mind that is a hallmark of classic legal education.

CRIMINAL LAW

Even though Criminal Law is the most familiar type of law to non-lawyers, some law schools do not make it a required topic. Thus, it may not be part of the first-year curriculum at your law school. But you should take the course at some point. It provides you with a primer on issues you have heard about all your life but may not really understand. Do you really know what larceny is? How about breaking and entering, or arson? What is the difference between homicide and manslaughter? These may sound easy, but as ever the law provides a mountain of de-tails and nuances that you must learn if you want to develop even a working knowledge of the topic (or at least enough knowledge to bluff your way through a social conversation).

Unlike Civil Procedure, which focuses on the procedural aspects of a case, Criminal Law focuses on the substantive law involved in a case, such as what proof you need to convict someone of the crime of mur-der. Because these are crimes (the violation of a law found in the statute books), the plaintiff is always the government. Criminal Law overlaps a bit with Constitutional Law when it deals with situations in which indi-vidual rights and the state's rights conflict with each other. It is here, for example, that you may read about the famous *Miranda* case, which re-quired the police to advise suspects of their right to have an attorney present before interrogation begins.

LEGAL RESEARCH AND WRITING

All the other first-year law school courses carry an inherent seriousness and dignity (after all, *Constitutional Law* is about as august as you can get). Legal Research and Writing, the poor stepchild of first-year classes, is the only truly practical course of the lot. It's fine to distinguish between arcane forms of land ownership, or memorize the difference between assault and battery, but these intellectual feats will do you little good in a few years when you are a brand-new associate slaving away in the law library. The skills you really need to make your mark when you graduate are the ability to ferret out information from the mounds of legal data available in a law library and the ability to write a cogent, well-reasoned memo. This is what you learn in a first-year Legal Research and Writing class.

The research and writing course is more amorphous than the other courses. In general, it consists of three segments:

- learning the basics of legal research through an introduction to the law library
- utilizing your new law library knowledge to research and write a legal memorandum
- presenting an oral argument to a moot court

In some schools this course is taught not by regular professors but by guest teachers who take time from their off-campus legal jobs. Sometimes upper-class law students are utilized as a cheap source of labor. The result is that the quality of teaching in the research and writing course can vary widely from school to school.

The Law Library

No matter who leads the class, learning your way around a law library can be a bit dry. It may be more exciting than memorizing the Dewey decimal system but less so than pontificating on civil rights to your "Con Law" professor. Still, chances are that if you've chosen to go to law school, you have at least some tendency to be a stickler for details and facts. In that case, learning to navigate among a new sea of information may prove a little exciting.

Case Books

The main kind of book found in law libraries is case books. They reprint judges' decisions in court cases going back before the birth of the United States. You will find every U.S. Supreme Court case and most federal district court and appeals court cases as well. For state court cases, usually only those of one or two of the highest state courts are readily available in print. The court decisions appear chronologically, lumped together by court. All the U.S. Supreme Court cases are in one enormous series of books. All the lower federal court decisions have their own series of volumes, as do the state supreme court cases. There are also many specialized categories, such as books covering just Bankruptcy Court or Tax Court cases. Each case begins with a brief introduction setting forth the basic facts and summarizing the rulings made by the court in that case.

Finding Relevant Cases

Because there have been so many court cases over the past two hundred years, it is a Herculean task to find and analyze salient ones when you are concerned with a particular legal concept. Being able to find all similar cases is the basic task of legal research. For example, perhaps a landlord sues a tenant for not paying the rent, but the tenant refuses to pay because the landlord's drunken brother-in-law accidentally knocked down half the apartment building with his bulldozer. If you need to know the likely outcome, you can start by looking at the lease itself. Chances are, the lease may not directly address the issue of destruction by an inebriated relative of the landlord. The next place to look is the statute books of the state where the incident took place. Again, the legislature has probably not passed a law specifically dealing with this issue. So you need to find out if such a situation has come up before, either in your area or in another state. If a judge faced virtually the same problem at some time in the past, the judge in *this* case will likely rule the same way. Thus, you need to find all similar cases. How on earth do you go through more than two hundred years of cases from fifty states and all federal courts? Well, that is where your legal research training will come in handy.

In the old days before computers, the primary research tool you relied on was the brief summaries of court decisions that appear at the beginning of the cases in most case books. These summaries are themselves categorized by topics, sub-topics, sub-sub-topics, and so on. You then review special guidebooks, organized by topics, that reprint each decision summary within each individual topic and sub-topic. Thus, in our example, you begin by looking in the guidebook under leases. You next find the sub-topic for nonpayment of rent, then move deeper to the sub-sub-topic of tenants' justification for nonpayment. Now look for a sub-sub-sub-topic of damage to the apartment and finally for the sub-sub-sub-sub-topic of destruction that is arguably the fault of the landlord. Here, you find short summaries of the handful of court decisions involving facts similar to our example. Only then will you actually look up some cases, read them, and see if they apply.

In the new world of computer databases, you let your fingers do the walking, as you access a computer database with thousands of court cases in its memory. Here, you might ask the computer to search for any cases that contain the words *lease, breach, rent, damage,* and *fault of landlord* within the same paragraph, and in a few seconds, it spits out the applicable case names and is ready to print out the cases for you. Be aware that this computer-aided research can be expensive and some law schools still rely on nonelectronic resources. At schools that have only recently joined the computer era, students may find that the long wait for computer access forces many to fall back on the printed page.

The process of searching for similar cases sounds relatively easy, but it isn't. There are so many cases and levels of courts, so many topics and variations of topics, that you can easily get lost trying to find your way around. The legal research course walks you through this apparent maze of information and introduces you to all the various types of cases and search tools so that you can drastically reduce the amount of time you spend looking things up.

Other Library Volumes

Of course, court cases aren't the only thing you'll find in a law library. There are volumes devoted just to statutory laws (federal laws and those of all fifty states) and to regulations (the interpretations of laws issued by federal and state government agencies). There are guidebooks to particular topics such as antitrust, environmental regulation, and taxation. These combine summaries of court cases and reprints of applicable laws and regulations with explanations of the topic. In addition, there are law journals, which publish scholarly articles by legal researchers. Legal treatises and encyclopedias simply discuss topics in a more traditional, straightforward way, with helpful footnotes listing leading cases on each point. In order to be able to fully utilize the law library, you must understand how to use all these types of tools.

Learning to fully utilize the law library can make a big difference in how good a lawyer you will be. One of the hardest lessons for a young law student to learn is that nobody really cares what *you* think about how to resolve a dispute. The only thing that matters is what a judge, a legislature, or an administrative agency (or perhaps a famous law professor) said on a similar topic. If you find a court decision supporting your idea, you may win the day. If you can't, you will probably lose. Cases dealing with similar facts are like gold in the legal world. Being able to quickly focus on similar cases is like money in the bank for a law student.

Legal Memoranda

After the introduction to the law library, you put your new knowledge to practical use by writing short legal memoranda. This is good practice because newly graduated lawyers often spend most of their time responding to bizarrely phrased inquiries from more senior attorneys. "What will happen," the partner will posit to the young associate, "now that a foreigner in the United States illegally ran a red light in a rented car, accidentally knocked over a fire hydrant that sprayed water all over our client's valuable Karmann Ghia convertible that was double-parked nearby, and ruined the rich Corinthian leather seats? Can we sue the foreigner in this state? What about the person who rented the car to the foreigner? What about the manufacturer of the fire hydrant? What exactly do we charge any of them with? What are we likely to recover if we win?" The associate then scurries away to the law library, researches the twenty or thirty legal issues buried in those questions, and comes up with possible answers. The answers are presented to the partner in the form of a legal memorandum from the associate to the partner. The memo begins by summarizing the facts and restating the questions. Then it summarizes the conclusions reached. The main body of the memo discusses each issue, point by point, listing the authority (statute, case, regulation, etc.) that serves as the basis for each of the associate's findings. The partner reviews the memo (and perhaps asks for more details or poses additional questions) before responding to the client who asked the original simple question: "Do I have a chance to recover if I bring a lawsuit over the damage to my lovely car?"

In the first-year writing course, students receive fairly esoteric queries (although perhaps not as convoluted as the one above), research the issues, and write memoranda on their conclusions. Grades depend on both the quality of the research and the clarity of the writing.

Moot Court

After dealing with memoranda, the first-year writing program usually concludes with writing trial briefs. The students then present their briefs to a pretend (or moot) court, made up of judges who are really upperclassmen or recent law school alumni. A trial brief is usually more research-oriented than a legal memorandum. Its job is to convince a judge to rule in your favor, by reviewing the other cases that support your argument. In this sense, a trial brief resembles a really long memo, a sort of final writing exam. Once the brief is written, however, you must move on to the oral presentation. As in a real court, you address the judges (who have read the briefs in advance) and try to present a winning summary of your position. The judges often interrupt the presentation to ask pointed and often unexpected questions. The presenter must think quickly, without much help from a script. For many, this public performance can be extremely unnerving. For the more theatrical types who intend to go into real-life litigation, this is like opening night for a play staring *them*. No matter how you view your moot court experience, it will no doubt prove to be one of your most vivid memories of the first year of law school. It sure beats reading three-hundred-year-old cases dealing with the nuances of inheriting real estate.

4

THE SECOND AND THIRD YEARS

Once you survive the first year of law school, you gain more freedom in your ability to select your courses. The first-year curriculum is largely predetermined for you, with little choice on your part. However, for the second and third years, you are pretty much on your own, and you can choose from whatever courses are available. This allows students who have already developed an interest in one particular aspect of law to specialize by taking all related courses that the school offers. Specializing is fine if you are convinced of your ultimate job goal, but taking a well-rounded course load is usually best.

Courses in the second and third years tend not to emphasize the Socratic teaching style as much as first-year courses do. The primary focus shifts from teaching a way of thinking to teaching particular topics. Some courses for upper-class students avoid the traditional classroom setting altogether. They may opt for more individualized formats (such as writing projects) where students have more control over how their time is spent.

UPPER-CLASS COURSES

Upper-class courses can focus on virtually any aspect of the legal world. A representative batch includes the following:

- Evidence
- Corporations

- Trusts and Estates
- Commercial Code
- Bankruptcy
- Antitrust
- Federal Tax
- Securities
- Labor Law
- Administrative Law
- Broadcast Regulation
- Entertainment Law
- Professional Responsibility
- Upper-class Writing Project

Evidence

Here you learn the rules of court (usually federal court, to avoid state-by-state anomalies) that govern the kinds of evidence you can present during a trial. If the defendant admitted doing some misdeed in writing, can you get by with presenting a photocopy, or do you need the original? Can you force the other side's accountant to divulge confidential information about the amount of money made last year? You will also learn about the hearsay rule, which is so complicated that it cannot be adequately summarized in a simple sentence, and about the even more complex exceptions to the general rule.

Corporations

Each state has its own laws governing corporations, the most popular form of entity used when setting up businesses in the United States. Understanding the laws that apply to corporations is vital to understanding the business world. Frequently, this course will focus on Delaware's corporate law, because that state has for some time been the most influential in setting corporate trends. Examples of topics covered here include how to set up a corporation, what rules govern its operation, what rights and duties come with being a stockholder, director, or officer of a corporation, and what special rules apply to lawsuits by and against corporations. The latest development in this area is a new business format, the limited liability company, which is a hybrid combining aspects of corporations and partnerships.

Trusts and Estates

Many people are familiar with the concept of writing a will, but few laymen appreciate the complex rules that govern how to properly sign a will and how they are interpreted. This course, which guides the novice through this specialized field, is highly practical, as it applies to almost everyone at some point. The course also focuses on trusts, which are separate legal entities that hold money donated by a person either during life or upon death. Trusts then distribute that money as the original donor instructed over a period of ten, twenty, even a hundred or more years. The cases in this course are often lively, as they all tend to involve children of rich families squabbling over the bundle that dad left to Fifi the upstairs maid or that mom left to Raoul, the gardener. You don't get much closer to soap opera in law school than in Trusts and Estates.

Commercial Code

All fifty states have adopted a virtually standard set of business laws called the Uniform Commercial Code, or the UCC. This set of laws is the basic rule book governing business affairs. It covers issues such as which language governs when the seller and the buyer each send out contracts containing conflicting minuscule provisions on the back. It also deals with how a seller can obtain some collateral for a debt owed by the buyer following a purchase. In the common occurrence of a customer paying for goods by check, the UCC establishes what each of the many parties involved in the processing of that check must do to avoid being left holding the bag if the check bounces. Even more so than many statutes, the UCC is fairly turgid and resists quick skimming by bored students. The course can be deadly dull at times but is indispensable if you plan on working in general business law.

Bankruptcy

The federal bankruptcy code is a world all to itself. It is a special subset of laws that only apply in bankruptcy situations, containing rules and procedures far different from most other legal settings. Once a person or business has declared bankruptcy, most other laws no longer apply, creditors have to ask the court for permission to be paid, and the bankruptcy court has amazingly wide discretion to decide what should happen. Not long ago, declaring bankruptcy was the absolutely last resort. It carried a public stigma that scared off many who might otherwise have made use of the concept. But now, bankruptcy has become simply another strategy option for troubled companies and individuals. The laws here are highly complex and confusing. It takes a skilled professor to add a little life to the proceedings.

Antitrust

When studying antitrust laws, you learn how the government regulates practices used by businesses trying to squeeze out smaller competitors. Since the turn of the century, the government has enforced some fairly strict rules forbidding the creation of monopolies in many businesses. These antitrust laws have evolved into a thick web of rules and regulations that affect all but the smallest companies. The exciting cases here are the older ones, where gigantic robber baron conglomerates were humbled before the power of the crusading government prosecutors. Somehow the more recent story of the forced breakup of AT&T doesn't have quite the same romantic air to it.

Federal Tax

Like trusts and estates, tax applies to everyone. The tax code is one of the most complicated portions of federal law. It is filled with general rules that have many significant exceptions and hundreds of exceptions to the exceptions, all of which you need to understand before you can decipher the tax effect of a transaction. Since everything you do in life (it seems) has some sort of tax impact, you'd better have at least a passing knowledge of the tax code. Otherwise, you may find it impossible to intelligently discuss a proposed business action with your client. One of the most annoying things about the federal tax course is that it uses the thickest, hardest-to-carry books of all: the huge federal tax code itself, plus an equally huge set of tax regulations. If the federal tax system is ever simplified, this course may become obsolete, but don't hold your breath.

Securities

Before the Great Depression, there were few, if any, regulations governing the sale of stocks and bonds (also known as securities), but the 1930s revealed some egregiously deceptive practices conducted by those promoting the sale of securities, and Franklin Roosevelt's New Deal quickly established stringent federal rules governing this activity. Most of those laws are still on the books and now are even more stringent than ever. The securities course winds through the morass of regulations that businesses must follow if they want to offer stock to the public and discusses the vast set of disclosure requirements that apply once a stock is publicly traded. Securities class can provide a look behind the curtain to see how big-league businesses gather investors and what can happen if they try to cut corners.

Labor Law

Virtually everyone will work for someone else at some time, and this makes Labor Law another practical course to have taken before graduation. Topics include employment contracts and union troubles, such as strikes, as well as noncompetition agreements, collective bargaining contracts, and sexual harassment claims. This field has burgeoned in importance over the last few decades, as disputes over the hiring and firing of employees have become almost as commonplace as slip-and-fall cases.

Administrative Law

This one sounds like a snoozer, and that impression is largely accurate. While legislatures pass laws, it is the inner government bureaucracies, the administrative agencies, which have to actually implement those laws. Each agency tends to have its own set of rules, called regulations. This course helps you understand the way these virtual fiefdoms operate. Don't take this in mid-afternoon; you'll tend to doze off.

Broadcast Regulation

Since we are all familiar with the media, this class, which surveys the laws governing broadcast and cable operations, tends to incite lively student disputes about how the government should (or should not) control this field. This area of law is changing rapidly, as new technologies and new laissez-faire government philosophies make decades-old concepts and practices obsolete. Equally relevant are the sidelights on free speech and obscenity issues, which have affected the media from the beginning.

Entertainment Law

Going beyond the scope of Broadcast Regulation, Entertainment Law covers a broader range of laws on newspapers, movies, books, and music as well as TV, cable, and radio. This course combines a lot of administrative law, constitutional law, and antitrust law, but places all these issues in the more interesting setting of the entertainment world. The subject matter tends to fascinate the star-struck of the student body, and the class can be far more interesting if some local celebrity occasionally serves as a guest lecturer or guest professor. In Harry's case, his Entertainment Law guest professor was Sumner Redstone, who was then already a local movie theater magnate but had yet to become one of the most powerful people in the industry as owner of Viacom.

Professional Responsibility

In addition to elective courses, most law schools require upperclassmen to take a course in professional ethics. Like many professionals, lawyers have their own professional rules and regulations, governing such things as how lawyers are actually licensed to practice and what they have to do to maintain their status as lawyers in good standing. Violating these rules can lead to professional discipline and even disbarment. Professional Responsibility teaches these rules. It can deal with fairly juicy topics such as what to do when you "know" your client committed the crime and how far you can go in using technicalities to mess up your opposition. While the concept of urging budding barristers to behave ethically is naturally commendable, many students view this course as something of a lark. The class is usually rather easy, and professors tend (despite their best intentions) not to devote as much energy to it as they do to other courses. Frankly, students tend to feel that this topic, even more so than the others in law school, will have very little direct impact on their future lives. The only immediate benefit they see is that most states require those wishing to be admitted as lawyers following graduation to pass a professional responsibility test. This course can serve as a fine preparation for that test.

Upper Class Writing Project

Finally, many law schools require upper-class students to prepare a writing project at some time during the second or third year. Similar to an undergraduate thesis or independent study program, this writing program allows you to proceed pretty much on your own once you receive faculty approval of your topic. In many ways, it is a grander version of the first-year writing assignments, involving deeper research. If you choose a topic that excites you, it can be fascinating to dig into the issue and formulate a cogent, well-thought-out analysis. Sometimes the most valuable part of this course is having your own preconceived conclusions altered by the information you dig up during your research. That is true learning.

OUTSIDE THE CLASSROOM

Beyond regular classroom courses and research programs, many law schools offer other activities that bridge the gap between academia and the outside world. These more eclectic activities provide some of the greatest opportunities for law students to gain experiences that will set them apart from the mass of their classmates.

Clinical Programs

A growing number of law schools now offer a form of internship called clinical programs. These provide students with direct exposure to the work environment in particular areas of law while they are still earning academic credits. Sometimes, students assist practicing attorneys working on actual trials or work for government agencies enforcing some of the laws covered in classroom study. Sometimes they help attorneys provide legal assistance to indigent clients. Naturally, the actual work done by the students in these settings is the most menial and low-level. Still, observing lawyers at work firsthand is a valuable learning experience. It is often far more rewarding than hours spent in the law library poring over some obscure point of theoretical procedure. Law school is sometimes criticized (correctly) as being too much a world unto itself, which does not properly prepare aspiring attorneys for the reality of legal practice. The intent of clinical programs is to help remedy that shortfall, and it is much to your advantage to make use of this option if it is offered.

Law Journals

Aside from courses and programs offered for academic credit, law schools also offer law-related extracurricular activities. Most law schools sponsor one or more publications operated and sometimes controlled by students. These publications may specialize in one particular legal field, but the most famous law school journal, the law review, covers any and all legal topics. Students "on law review" are those who help publish the law school's academic journal, which publishes issues about four to six times per year. Professors or other legal scholars, who are often trying out new, cutting-edge ideas in legal theory, usually write the articles.

In essence, the students on law review have a separate almost full-time job on top of the always imposing demands of keeping up with normal law school classes. Only students in the top echelon of scholastic rankings are invited to join the law review. Most schools allow students who are not granted such an honor to compete in a writing assignment to try to earn an invitation. Because students on law review have an oppressive workload in addition to the normal course work, they tend to be the most stressed-out people on campus. The grind can be draining, but the prestige is great.

The senior law review staff members edit the journal, performing tasks similar to that of the editor of any professional publication. They select article topics and manage the publication through the various stages of preparation for publication. The junior members of the law review spend their time performing the far more mundane work of cite checking, which can be a task of mind-numbing drudgery. As noted in Chapter 3, most legal thinking consists of drawing new conclusions from old precedents. Thus, in a law review article, the author will constantly back up statements with footnotes referencing the sources (citations or cites) of the assertions. The cite checker must review each source to make sure that it truly does support the author's statement and that it precisely follows a maddeningly intricate format. While on law review, students usually publish at least one article themselves. With a far larger audience than the run-of-the-mill class paper, a law review article can bring the student author a fair measure of notoriety. This is a valuable commodity when trying to compete for professional advancement following graduation.

Law review is traditionally the most prestigious activity at law school. Making law review at a respected law school may, in and of itself, guarantee you a decent job upon graduation. At some lower-ranked schools, it may virtually be a requirement if you intend to get a high-profile job. Being on law review will add a sparkling jewel to your resume forever and always set you apart from your less-honored classmates. The hard work also creates a "wartime" camaraderie with your fellow students on law review that can lead to lasting friendships, or to contacts that may prove valuable in years to come as your law review colleagues move on to positions of power after graduation.

While the benefits of being on law review are undeniable, you should carefully consider whether the crushing work burden of the position is worth the honor (if you are offered it). The time crunch of working on law review may cause you to ignore regular classes. This may depress your grade-point average over time, which looks bad even for law review stars. If you are not hoping to land a job among the cream of the private legal community, you may not need to undertake work on law review to get where you want to be.

We both decided that law review was not for us. Even though we each felt we could have been eligible for law review based on our grades, we each concluded that we were busy enough, thank you, so we did not pursue it. Adding a new load of chores from law review just did not seem the smartest way to use one of the most precious commodities in law school—time.

Aside from law review, there are other ways to set yourself apart from the mass of other job seekers in your class. For one thing, the law review is usually not the only journal published by the law school. There may be more specialized publications, such as those dealing with antitrust or environmental topics, which are easier to join. These are frequently less demanding and may be more in tune with your interests. Finally, of course, you can simply concentrate on your courses. Maintaining an impressive grade-point average is still the most basic way of making yourself attractive to employers upon graduation.

JOINT DEGREE PROGRAMS

When you graduate from law school, you earn a juris doctor (J.D.) degree. Some students may also wish to obtain another degree to complement the basic J.D. There are advanced law degrees, such as Master of Taxation, which allow specialization in particular fields of law. You may also expand your education by obtaining degrees from other academic disciplines, such as business administration, economics, urban planning, or social work. Usually, these extra degrees are earned separately, either before or after the three-year law school stint. However, more and more law schools and universities are allowing students to earn multiple degrees simultaneously through joint degree programs. In these, students can earn two degrees in a shorter time than it would normally take to earn them separately.

A joint degree program can be perfect for students who know precisely what field they wish to enter. For example, a law school graduate with an M.B.A. is immediately more marketable than one with just a J.D. in the eyes of employers looking for business lawyers. However, those who are not so certain as to their future endeavors might want to think twice before committing themselves to the time and financial requirements of a joint degree program.

If a joint degree program appeals to you, be sure to thoroughly investigate potential law schools before you apply. Along with the usual process of evaluating law schools (discussed in Chapters 10–12), you will also need to check out the other degree programs at your target schools and learn how the joint degree program actually operates.

5

MOVING FROM LAW STUDENT TO LAWYER

O nce three years of law school classes and exams are over, you may have a law degree, but you are not yet fully a lawyer. There are still a few hurdles left before you can begin practicing as an attorney. One task is to pass yet another exam, called the bar exam, in order to receive a license to practice law. Aside from that, your primary hurdle is, of course, finding a job as a lawyer. The way to prepare for this transition from law student to lawyer is to find law-related jobs during summer vacations from law school.

SUMMER JOBS DURING LAW SCHOOL

While many law students spend their few moments of free time daydreaming about their future as Supreme Court justices or world-famous trial lawyers, the reality is that even the most distinguished legal career needs to start somewhere near the bottom. For most law students, the first job in law is a summer job in some remote corner of the legal world. Theoretically, law students should have the opportunity for summer jobs during two years before graduation (the summers between first and second and second and third years), but for many it doesn't work out that way.

First-Year Jobs

The reality of the marketplace is that many law students find it extremely difficult to obtain a paying law-related job in the summer after the first year of law school. The main reason is supply and demand. Because so many second-year law students are also out looking for jobs, there is not much room left for the hordes of first-year students. Although first-year students may feel they are full of legal knowledge, they are markedly less sophisticated about the law than their second-year fellow students. First-year students have been immersed in the basics of law, which rarely have any immediate applicability to practical law work. Second-year students have spent a year delving into more specialized topics, gaining some modest familiarity with the basic terms tossed around by practicing attorneys. On a practical level, second-year students already have a set of law school grades that rank them by some measure of merit. They are also just months away from becoming a resource employers really seek: graduates looking for full-time jobs.

Consequently, the few first-year students who do land summer jobs in law tend to wind up with extremely low-level positions. Some do not even get regular wages. The experience truly is valuable, especially for those who have little experience in the work force, but finding first-year summer law jobs is pretty much a process of chasing them down on your own.

Second-Year Jobs

The summer after second year is quite different. Suddenly, the roles are reversed, and it is the employers who come looking for the students. Near the midpoint of the second year, law firms, companies, and some government agencies send recruiters to the major nearby law schools in order to search for summer legal talent. Traditionally, students submit their resumes in advance to those employers they find interesting. The employers then pick which students they wish to meet when the recruiter is in town. On the appointed day, the recruiters will set up shop on or near campus and engage in marathon interview sessions with eager second-year students. After digesting the information (and calling back some prospects for a second round of interviews), the employers will offer summer positions to a small number of lucky students, who then have a set time to decide which offer to accept.

Come summer, the student (now called a law clerk) will arrive, anxious but excited, at the office. What actually happens during the summer clerkship varies widely. In the not-too-distant past, the standard routine for large big-city firms was to have an almost nonstop summer party for the clerks. Work assignments were not overly burdensome, and the clerks were kept on a social whirlwind of concerts, sporting events, beach parties, and get-togethers at the homes of the full-time lawyers. Best of all, the pay was usually good ($1,500 per week at the largest Manhattan firms). The summer clerk for the first time began to taste the sweet results of all that studying.

That sort of practice still continues at some firms, but many law firms, downsizing like other businesses, had to cut out much of the fluff some years ago. Many employers, especially the government agencies, never went in for the hoopla even in the old days. A more common current scenario is to have the clerks enjoy a few organized social events but spend most of their time actually working.

Most summer clerks carry out elementary research and writing assignments, to assist young associates. There is much library time and much preparation of routine documents. Still, the students get to see the real world of law up close and personal. Many employers will rotate summer clerks in and out of different departments so that more staff members can size up them up and so that the clerks receive a more balanced set of assignments.

From the point of view of employers, summer clerks are in the position of minor league ballplayers. The employers see what the students can do and decide which, if any, should be invited back to the big time, after graduation. Of course, the students do much the same thing. They decide if they want to come back to the same office after graduation. Usually, by summer's end, the employer will have made offers of full-time jobs to a select few. Most students wait to decide whether to accept an offer until they are back in school for the third and final year of law school.

Second-year clerkships are a wonderful way to try out possibilities. You can indulge yourself and try a summer job in some legal field you know little about but find interesting. Similarly, you may opt to take a summer job far from home in an alluring city, just to see if you find it to your liking. The beauty of second-year summer jobs is that they are like blind dates. If it works—great; you can plan to get together again soon. If it doesn't, well, you weren't planning to get married anyway, and the experience was valuable.

THIRD-YEAR INTERVIEWS FOR
POST-GRADUATION JOBS

Once back on campus for the third year, you will have a new round of interviews late in the fall. The process here is virtually the same as the interviews during second year, but these interviews are more serious. They are for real *jobs,* and both sides are far more circumspect in how they present themselves. The time for experimentation is gone.

When Harry was a student, he received an offer for full-time employment from the firm where he clerked in the summer after his second year. It felt like having money in the bank to sit on that offer and still go through the interview process during the third year. Eventually, Harry chose to accept the offer from his summer firm, and he could then rest somewhat easily for the rest of the final year of law school, knowing a job was waiting after graduation.

One alternative to heading right into a permanent position is serving for one or two years as an assistant (clerk) to a sitting judge. The new graduate will perform research tasks for the judge and may even get to compose the judge's written decisions. Capturing a short-term judicial clerkship also requires rounds of interviews, and it can help open doors to a full-time job when the clerkship ends. A judicial clerkship after graduation is the option Chris chose, feeling it was the best way to develop some legal expertise and a better sense of the legal profession before committing to a permanent position. He had also received a job offer from his summer employer, which could be held open during Chris's judicial clerkship. On top of all that, he still went through the third-year job interview process in order to examine all possible avenues.

AFTER GRADUATION: THE BAR EXAM

Eventually, the third year of law school ends, you graduate, and school is over. Now what? Those with job offers usually go right to work. Those with no offers make new attempts at finding a job opening in the legal world (by mass mailing of resumes and old-fashioned networking). However, there is one last law school–related event that all new graduates must face—taking the bar exam.

The J.D. degree you earn upon graduation does *not* mean you can go right out and practice law. First, you must pass an extremely detailed test, the bar exam, given by each state's bar (association of lawyers). Passing the bar exam of a state earns you a license to practice law in that state. In general, you must pass the bar exam in every state in which you want to practice. Bar exams usually last two (or even three) days, and are given a few times each year. The most popular testing time is at midsummer, to take into account the many who graduate each June.

Preparing and Applying

You must apply for the bar exam months in advance, perhaps even before you know where you will be working after graduation. The application process is lengthy, intrusive, annoying, and often frustrating. You may be asked to list all your addresses and all your jobs since high school. You may need to obtain references from three to five people (such as professors or lawyers). You may even need to state whether you've ever been a member of the Communist party.

After the application comes the preparation for the test itself. Many graduates prepare for the bar exam by taking professional preparatory courses, which review the topics covered by the exam and its format. Some preparatory classes run for a month or two before the exam, while others are crash courses in the week before the test.

The bar exam is usually broken into three main segments. The first is the multistate portion, consisting of multiple-choice questions covering general "national" laws shared by virtually all states. This portion is the same, in essence, wherever you take the bar exam. The second section is the state portion, which tests you on the specific laws of one individual state. This portion combines multiple-choice questions and several essays that are similar to law school final exams. The third portion, a short national exam on professional ethics, is much less difficult than the other two and is usually given at a different time than the other two segments.

Studying for the bar exam may be the first time you *ever* study the specific laws of your own state, because many law schools teach only the general laws followed nationwide. Studying your local state laws can be a bit disconcerting; you may find out, for example, that your state does not follow the majority of other states in particular legal theories. If for no other reason, boning up on your own state's special laws is a good reason to take one of the professional preparatory courses.

Taking the Test

The bar exam itself is extremely draining. As you go in, you will probably feel like a soggy sponge, overflowing with information that spills out of you. The fear of failing this exam can be even worse than the fear concerning law school exams, because the bar exam is truly the final exam with the highest stakes. Pass rates fall in the 75–80 percent range, and the difficulty of the bar exam varies greatly from state to state. Chances are, you will stumble out of the bar exam feeling as if you failed miserably (don't obsess over it, *most* people feel that way). And you need to wait months before you find out the results. But by the time you do, you will hopefully be hard at work at a new job.

The End of the Beginning

Eventually, some blandly written notice from the state bar association will arrive in the mail, announcing simply that you passed or did not pass. If you failed, you can take the test again, but that will prevent you from being formally admitted as a practicing attorney for months. This leaves you in legal purgatory, where you are severely limited in what you can do on your own as a lawyer. Worse yet, your prospective employer may even revoke your job offer!

If you passed, you then wait a bit longer until the day finally arrives when you are formally admitted as a lawyer. Frequently, the admission ceremony will occur in some ornate locale with a local legal celebrity serving as the master of ceremonies. Sometimes, the new lawyers parade up to the stage one by one, to be sworn in and receive their bar admission papers. Sometimes, the entire group simply stands up and takes the oath en masse.

And then, it's all over. You are really a lawyer. This is what you wanted all those years ago when you decided to apply to law school. Congratulate yourself. You have worked your way through a giant maze of law boards, law school applications, three years of classes, summer jobs, graduation, bar applications, and the bar exam. Many colleagues will have dropped out of the process along the way, but you made it! Chances are, you will not have too long to savor this triumph. Most new lawyers will have to scurry back to the office. By then the whole process will be somewhat anticlimactic. Law school will already be fading from your memory, and even the bar exam will be old news. After all, it's finally time to get to work.

6

WHERE DO LAWYERS WORK?

If you break your arm, you would not ask an eye doctor to fix it. People understand that many medical practitioners are specialists. However, the same distinction is not readily made for the legal profession, even though lawyers specialize in much the same way. This misunderstanding comes largely from the heavy emphasis given to trial lawyers in news stories involving attorneys and from the portrayals of lawyers in the popular media. Simply put, the general population lacks understanding of what lawyers actually do. The truth is that many lawyers rarely set foot in a courtroom.

In order to make an educated choice about whether to pursue a legal career, you should understand the structure and nature of the legal profession. This chapter and the next discuss two central issues: where lawyers work and what types of work they do.

The principal places employing lawyers are

- private law firms
- private businesses
- government

PRIVATE LAW FIRMS

The best-known type of lawyer is the one who works for a law firm. These are, in essence, private business men and women whose fortunes, like others in the private sector, rise and fall depending on the number and nature of the customers (clients) the firm attracts. Within private law firms, the essential distinction is between partners and associates.

Partners and Associates

In a nutshell, partners are management and associates are labor. A partner's take-home pay is frequently tied to the profits of the firm and consequently may fluctuate greatly. Partners are literally stockholders in the law firm, with an ownership interest that cannot be terminated without some form of buyout. Partners control the operation of a firm, but they also must handle numerous administrative chores that often eat up valuable time they would prefer to devote to lawyering.

Associates, on the other hand, are simply employees, usually paid a set annual salary and subject to termination at any time. Each year, the partners decide which, if any, associates deserve to be elevated to partner status. Associates tend to become partners, if at all, largely on the basis of their ability to bring in significant clients of their own. In many firms, associates who are not chosen to become a partner within five or six years are let go.

Most lawyers in private firms charge an hourly rate for their services, with any one lawyer's rate depending on such factors as seniority and status. Thus, the cost of having a will drawn up depends upon the billing rate of the lawyer who does the work. The more hours an attorney works and can bill out to a client, the more money comes into the firm. Associates benefit only indirectly from billing many hours. It really helps during annual salary reviews, but an associate's pay remains constant throughout the year. A partner's salary, however, is directly tied to the revenue received from his or her clients for billed hours.

Law firms can be analyzed by dividing them into three general size categories: large, medium, or small. Each has its own pluses, minuses, and idiosyncrasies.

Large Law Firms

What constitutes a "large" firm depends upon where you look. In New York City a large firm can easily have over three hundred attorneys (not counting the branch offices in, say, Washington, London, Milan, and Rangoon). In a city like Boise, Idaho, a large firm will rarely have more than thirty lawyers. Nevertheless, large firms tend to act the same no matter where they are. They luxuriate in the sense of bigness. They can be found in the tallest, most opulent office buildings in town. They overwhelm you with ornate trappings such as expensive furniture and fully stocked food courts. They know they are the big players in town and rarely let outsiders forget it, such as when the aloof receptionist pays little attention to unknown guests or when clients receive whopping bills for relatively simple legal procedures. Large firms operate like large corporations, in both a good and a bad sense. One branch of a large firm frequently has no idea what the other parts of the same firm are doing. Yet large firms are more than the sum of the individuals who work there, carrying an identity that often sells itself.

Advantages

Just like nonlaw businesses, a large law firm has many advantages over its smaller competitors. Largeness brings depth, and large firms can deal with complex legal issues without having to stoop to consulting with outsiders. They have tremendous resources, both in library material and practical experience, that are valuable when combating a powerful opponent. Large firms often have a twenty-four-hour word-processing center. The typists can easily turn three dictation tapes dropped off by a bleary-eyed associate at midnight into a nearly finished seventy-five-page memo ready for review when the supervising partner arrives at the crack of dawn. Because large firms can afford it (that is, they have very rich clients who will pay for it), their lawyers can take the time to delve into nuances of the law often overlooked by more modest colleagues.

Lawyers in large law firms also receive training as to the "right" way to do everything, not just the quick and simple way that smaller firms may prefer so as to not run up humongous charges to the client. A large firm's attention to detail results in big fees and provides the associates with unrivaled training. They learn about a breadth of topics other lawyers never deal with during an entire career. There is no denying the buzz that newly minted associates get when, six months after lounging around law school in grungy jeans, they find themselves in flashy new suits, working on highly confidential cases involving the most important people in town.

There is also no denying the allure of a big firm's big salary. Lawyers hired out of law school by a big firm can often start at annual salaries that equal or exceed that of an experienced small-town solo practitioner. Just like star athletes coming out of college, young lawyers often cannot resist the siren song of a hefty paycheck right up front. It is nice to be able to pay off those student loans faster than expected, but law school graduates need to remember that bigger does not always mean better. Large firms have their share of disadvantages to keep in mind.

Disadvantages

One of the problems in a large firm is the impersonal nature of the work atmosphere. Because there are simply too many people, lawyers in large firms often have trouble developing any camaraderie outside of their departments. You may never see lawyers from other floors except at formal office functions. This reduces the sense of pulling together for a common good and accentuates the feeling of everyone being out for themselves.

New associates at large firms usually spend quite some time (easily up to a year or two) squirreled away in the law library. There they perform the legal equivalent of working at McDonald's: looking up cases. They may spend hours or days researching some arcane legal point that is part of some larger, never fully explained case strategy and that may not even be used at all. You may be working on the most exciting legal case in town, but it will be hard to impress your nonlawyer friends with stories about your two days' examining exceptions to the hearsay rule.

Perhaps the roughest part of working at a large firm, especially for new lawyers, is the tendency to feel you are in the legal equivalent of a sweat shop. You may be required to work an oppressive amount of hours and hardly ever have contact with clients. Worse yet, there is often a deliberate scheme by partners to treat young associates as disposable cannon fodder. A large firm cannot possibly keep all the new lawyers it hires each year. Therefore, competition is fierce among new recruits to prove themselves better than the rest before they are winnowed out and dumped after slaving for a few years in the law library. The rejects will then be replaced by a new batch of fresh-faced graduates, hypnotized by the bright lights of the big city.

Small Law Firms

Just as location helps determine how large a firm must be to be considered "large," it also determines which firms are classified as "small."

In major metropolitan centers small firms may have fifty attorneys, whereas in provincial outposts two- and three-lawyer firms are common. In many ways, the small firm is the direct opposite of the large firm. Offices may be found in revamped private homes with drafty windows and suspect plumbing. On-site research material may be limited to an infrequently updated set of the local state statutes, and the support staff may be minuscule. The lawyer's time can often be taken up with run-of-the-mill mechanics, such as sending out copies of documents.

Advantages

Lawyers at small firms tend to be generalists, able to handle a wide range of issues. As with general practitioners in the medical field, this breadth of experience is admirable, but modern times tend to demand expertise in specialized areas. Lawyers in small firms sometimes become anachronisms because without specialization they cannot attract sizable new clients.

On the other hand, new lawyers at small firms get immediate client contact, which is the only way they can be true counselors rather than research machines. Early in their careers they may make court appearances, negotiate leases, or sit in on conferences with clients. This provides the novice attorney with invaluable practical training.

Another positive aspect of small firms is the close-knit nature of the workplace. Everyone knows everyone else. Lawyers feel comfortable walking down the hall and seeking the assistance of a fellow attorney who may know more than they do about a current legal issue. The atmosphere is far less formal than at big firms. Less wealthy clients will not have to wonder if half of their bill is going to pay for the new French chandelier in the lobby.

Disadvantages

On the down side, the cases at small firms are often mundane and routine, lacking the allure of a multimillion-dollar takeover campaign or a celebrity court case. Also, because clients are less willing to accept gargantuan bills, small firms often cannot afford to investigate all the possible angles of a matter, preferring instead to "just get it done." The client is happy with the reduced fee, but the small-firm lawyer may miss the chance to learn about some legal intricacies that could prove helpful in future situations.

Worst of all, a lawyer in a small firm might work almost as many hours as colleagues in larger firms do, while earning a fraction of the large-firm salary. Small-firm lawyers must contend with the stark financial realities of small-firm economics. They are always at risk of suffering economic trauma whenever a major client is lost or one of the partners leaves the firm.

Medium-Sized Law Firms

Advantages

Medium-sized law firms frequently combine the best and the worst of the characteristics described in the preceding sections. A medium-sized firm can be fairly informal and friendly yet large enough to handle a sophisticated group of clients with challenging problems. It can also provide a constant stream of bread-and-butter cases that provide ample training in the legal basics. Specialization is feasible to an extent, and thus a lawyer can develop a measure of expertise that is marketable, either in attracting clients to the current firm or in moving up to the big leagues.

Some medium-sized firms fill unique niches. These boutique firms may be highly specialized and only deal with one or two particular fields, such as bankruptcy or entertainment law. Unless they are in a sizable metropolis, firms that handle only a few areas of law cannot generate enough business to support a large staff of lawyers, but a smaller city can probably support a few boutique firms consisting of a few highly specialized attorneys.

Disadvantages

A medium-sized firm's major problem tends to be schizophrenia. The firm may not be satisfied with just being a stable player in the local legal marketplace. It may not really know if it is an up-and-coming large firm or an overblown small firm due for downsizing.

Moving Between Firms

Chances are great that if you go into private practice, you will move back and forth between types of firms during your legal career. Harry, for example, started out at one of the largest law firms in Jacksonville, Florida, but after two years he moved to a medium-sized firm in

Boston. He was not alone in this; within the first ten years after graduation, almost every one of Harry's law school friends who went into private practice also changed jobs.

The movement of lawyers between firms is not just a one-way street. Somewhat similar to Harry's history, some lawyers who start out as overpaid bonus babies at megafirms often bail out (voluntarily or otherwise) and are snapped up by smaller firms anxious to take advantage of the superior training a large firm provides. On the other hand, a small-firm lawyer who develops a strong expertise (and a client base that will follow along) can easily move up to become a big cheese at a much larger firm. It is the norm among lawyers to shift jobs more than once during a career, so don't worry that your first job out of law school will decide the course of the rest of your professional life.

PRIVATE BUSINESSES

Although a private law firm is the most widely known place to find working lawyers, there is an important second segment in the world of private lawyering: in-house lawyers in private business, also known as corporate counsel. Partners in private law firms are, in essence, business executives running their own companies. In-house lawyers, on the other hand, are just employees, working for the boss.

Many private businesses easily tire of paying outside lawyers hundreds of dollars an hour, so they hire their own company lawyers to do the same work for a fraction of the price. In-house lawyers often perform the same types of work as attorneys in private law firms, but they do not bill clients, because their client is the business they work for. They get paid a straight salary, just as everyone else at the company does.

Not needing to worry over the amount of billable hours, in-house counsel can, at least theoretically, spend as much or as little time as is needed to resolve an issue. In-house lawyers work shoulder-to-shoulder with the business executives, and so they develop an understanding of business operations that most lawyers in private law firms cannot touch. Successful in-house lawyers sometimes become part of the corporate management team itself.

While working as an in-house lawyer provides many benefits, the simple truth is that most legal superstars find it more rewarding (both personally and economically) to operate independently in private law firms. In-house lawyers, fairly or not, are sometimes considered second-stringers by their colleagues in private law firms. In fact, they often do not have the breadth of expertise that lawyers in large law firms do. Consequently, many companies with in-house lawyers will farm out the really big cases to private law firms, leaving the less flashy work for the company lawyers.

Despite the sometimes lower salary and somewhat lower prestige of in-house counsel, the position offers an often overlooked but highly satisfying compromise. It allows exposure to a healthy range of legal issues while eliminating the pressure of generating fees-paying clients. With many businesses lamenting the high legal fees charged by private law firms, in-house lawyering promises to be a burgeoning trend that may help to bring legal fees (and salaries) down from the stratosphere.

GOVERNMENT

Once you leave the world of private lawyers behind, the settings where other lawyers work begin to look quite different. The largest group of lawyers working outside of private law firms and businesses is found in the public sector—government.

Every government agency, be it the U.S. Department of State, the state sewer commission, or the local zoning board, has lawyers working for it. The work of these lawyers affects everyone. They draft rules and regulations, and interpret the law in ways that add specifics to the general laws passed by legislatures. However, the salaries earned by government lawyers rarely match those earned by colleagues at even medium-sized private law firms. Thus, government lawyers are often in the interesting position of dealing regularly with, and holding great power over, colleagues who earn far more than they do.

Most government lawyers perform the same types of work private-sector lawyers do, with their agency serving as their client. The most significant difference between public and private lawyers is that when representing their agency in criminal cases, government lawyers cannot, by definition, be defense attorneys but rather must always be the prosecutors, leading the government's charge against the accused.

One unfortunate fact of life for government lawyers is that they often have workloads as heavy as any private law counterpart but earn a lower salary. As a consequence, only certain types of people are attracted to government service. Some ambitious types see government work as a stepping-stone to holding public office themselves. Those who are truly public-spirited try hard to serve the public good without expecting a large salary. Some others simply prefer the sometimes reduced stress and fewer hours involved in working for government.

The most important public lawyers, of course, are those who become politicians. The appeal of the power and fame of holding public office is closely akin to the appeal of the legal profession itself, and thus it is little wonder that so many pass back and forth between the two worlds.

OTHER ALTERNATIVES

Most law school graduates wind up working for law firms, corporations, or some branch of government, but there are many other alternative positions that lawyers can fill, such as the following:

- law professors
- arbitrators/mediators
- legal aid lawyers
- lobbyists
- business executives
- legal assistants
- researchers
- journalists

Law Professors

Lawyers excited about the intellectual aspects of the law can find a refuge in the world of academia and teach new generations of law students. Law professors can exert great influence over the law and public policy debates by writing scholarly law review articles that suggest legal remedies the mainstream may not yet have considered. They also are able to personally mold future lawyers by providing law students with their first real exposure to the profession. On the other hand, legal academics often lead an insular existence, largely untouched by the jarring verities of life in the real world.

Arbitrators/Mediators

In contrast, arbitrators, mediators, and other dispute resolution professionals are far more in touch with day-to-day concerns. Dispute resolution services provide a forum for airing grievances and allow parties to reach a settlement outside of court. In these settings, lawyers use their abilities to ferret out details and negotiate compromises. In this manner, the parties can reach reasonable solutions in a manner far less expensive and combative than is likely in the open warfare of the courtroom. The astronomical cost of litigation has led more and more parties facing a lawsuit to make use of these services. Many observers of the legal world expect the popularity of dispute resolution services to increase steadily in the years to come.

Legal Aid Lawyers

Some law school graduates decide to devote their energies to aiding those who would not otherwise receive much legal assistance. Lawyers working for legal aid societies provide counsel to indigent clients who normally cannot pay for quality legal services. These lawyers perform an invaluable service, but they must contend with minimal resources, oppressive workloads, and marginal salaries.

Lobbyists

Somewhat less noble, but far more powerful, are legal lobbyists who advocate for their clients' positions directly to legislators and government officials who can truly make a difference. Some lobbyists work for public entities (such as Common Cause, the NAACP, or the NRA), advocating for the political agendas of their organizations. Others openly pursue the goals of a private interest such as an industry or a union. In their own way, these lobbyists help to mold and shape legislation nearly as much as the legislators on whom they practice their wiles.

Business Executives

Working as a business executive (not an in-house counsel) is another intriguing alternative to the traditional practice of law. Legal issues are often paramount in the decisions of a company, and legal training provides an ample background in negotiations. Business executives with law degrees have highly valued skills that may make them appealing to any forward-thinking business. Some old-fashioned tycoons may feel that lawyers-turned-executives do not have the inner toughness to navigate the shaky seas of private enterprise. But the fact is that private-firm lawyers bring with them the experience of having run a business: their own law firm.

Legal Assistants

Farther out on the fringes of the legal universe are less familiar fields for those with law degrees. Graduates unwilling to fully enter the legal rat race might find a simpler refuge in the role of a law librarian, legal researcher, or paralegal. These professionals work with and around lawyers and the law but not actually as lawyers.

Researchers

Publishers of legal material (periodicals, research aids, and textbooks) require the aid of lawyers to keep their materials relevant and up-to-date. This type of job is perfectly suited for those who love the technical nature of ever-changing legal rules but have difficulty dealing with clients.

Journalists

Finally, more and more in our litigious society, the world of journalism requires an army of lawyers to help interpret the legal shenanigans all around us. After all, the dwindling few among us who have yet to go to law school need someone to translate the legal jargon that so often fills the news.

7

WHAT DO LAWYERS DO?

Where lawyers work is an important factor in differentiating between the many types of attorneys, but even more significant is understanding what different types of lawyers do. A lawyer could move between private law firms, private businesses, and government, and still do much the same type of work. However, it is very unlikely that over the course of a career a lawyer would ever change the *type* of law he or she practices.

There is a vast array of types of law practice by which attorneys can be divided into identifiable groups. There are numerous specialties, sub-specialties, and sub-sub-specialties, but the primary division, especially in private practice, is between corporate lawyers and litigators.

CORPORATE LAWYERS

Corporate law is a catch-all term that encompasses almost every aspect of business. To understand what corporate lawyers do, just think about what a business does. Chances are, you will find a corporate lawyer behind the scenes, orchestrating the moves. For example, imagine that you want to start your own business. Is a corporation, a partnership, or a joint venture best for you? Ask your friendly corporate lawyer, who will tell you about the pluses and minuses of S corporations, C corporations, limited partnerships, general partnerships, limited liability companies, and limited liability partnerships. To properly form any of these, you will need a corporate lawyer to prepare the papers.

Now you may need outside investors to sink money into your new venture. How will the money come in, and what rights will the investors have? You need some documents to spell this out. Perhaps you would rather be financed through bank loans. Are the guaranties and pledges of collateral that the bank insists on right for you? Call your corporate lawyer.

Once you have money, you are ready to start doing business. Now you need contracts with suppliers and arrangements with customers, not to mention distributor agreements and sales representative documents. Don't forget your employees. What about employment contracts, confidentiality agreements, health care plans, and profit-sharing arrangements? You probably can't come up with all these on your own. Call your corporate lawyer.

Once your business is doing well, it may be time to consider franchising your operation or entering into licensing deals with foreign companies. Oh, did anyone mention there is a whole stack of government regulations that applies to your business? You are complying with them all, aren't you? Not sure? Better call . . . you know who.

You get the idea. Virtually any step a business takes requires some form of legal analysis and support. A struggling new business may not be able to afford to have a lawyer, even a small-firm lawyer, handle each of these aspects. On the other hand, an ongoing business may be able to handle a lot of the mundane day-to-day legal issues with their own staff but still need corporate specialists to handle the unusual events and the unexpected crises.

A central attribute of corporate lawyers is that they do not live and breathe adversarial combat. Their main goal is not to defeat someone but rather to accomplish something (albeit for their client's advantage, of course!). Thus, while litigation attracts competitive types (such as the ex-football fullback or the former top-ranked tennis pro), corporate law attracts more conciliatory yet persistent types (such as the former president of the school debating team). The ideal corporate lawyer is the tough negotiator, who knows all the inside angles and obtains a significant concession from the other side, which doesn't even realize it gave one because it doesn't know the law as well.

Spotting Trouble in Advance

Corporate lawyers tend to spend a fair amount of time drafting documents. However, they also frequently serve as business advisers (almost as silent partners). Almost any corporate lawyer can set up a new simple corporation in a day. A top lawyer's real value comes from anticipating problems that business people haven't considered and from restructuring a deal to obtain an unexpected advantage or to avoid possible problems in the future.

Harry, a corporate lawyer from the start, has received numerous "simple" one-page agreements from confident clients over the years, along with a modest request to "just look this over and let me know if it's okay." To the client's shock and dismay, a day or so later Harry often sends back a five-page comment letter and a revised draft of the agreement that runs ten pages. Part of this scenario (all too common among corporate lawyers) comes from an attorney's inbred urge to ramble on and add staggering layers of detail. When faced with simple prose ("Joe sells his widget to Mary"), lawyers will often not rest until they have added cumbersome triplets ("Joe, on behalf of his heirs, successors, and representatives, hereby sells, transfers, and assigns all of his right, title, and interest in a class-Z widget, model number GZA5568903, to Mary").

Beyond simply adding boilerplate wording, what the corporate lawyer is doing with the lengthy revised draft is using the ability to troubleshoot. Lawyers are trained to anticipate all the things that can go *wrong* in a deal, whereas businesspeople tend to concern themselves with how things work when everything is fine. Thus, a plan to have a company's salespeople drum up business in a new territory looks to the business executive like a simple question of what types of product to sell, what kinds of client to target, and how much commission should be paid. The lawyer, considering the same plan, conjures up nightmares of salesmen stealing customers and confidential information from the business, or pocketing commissions on sales that are later canceled because of faulty goods. They imagine customers who get angry and sue the business over the inflated promises made by the sales staff only interested in making sales, not in serving customers. This is followed, in the lawyer's mind, by images of salespeople making bogus commission claims for sales obtained by others and then charging the company with unlawful termination when they are told to take a hike. Lawyers respond to these fears, when drafting documents, by cramming in a hundred provisions designed to protect the business from every possible contingency. The novice lawyer is terrified by the panoply of things that can go wrong and tries to address them all in excruciating detail. The experienced lawyer, with a better sense of the real world of business, provides for the most likely risks and uses catch-all language to protect against the unlikely events. The seasoned attorney knows all too well that, if left to the lawyers, hardly any deal would ever get done because both sides would be too scared of potential liability to ever reach a compromise. In addition, most businesses simply cannot pay the legal fees needed to draft documents that protect against everything.

Advantages and Disadvantages

Practicing in the field of corporate law has several advantages. It is relatively easy on the blood pressure, it allows you to understand how business really works (something too few lawyers understand when they begin), and it gives you a sense of accomplishment when some new enterprise you counseled takes off and becomes a local powerhouse. Different types of people enjoy different types of personal interaction, but from Harry's point of view, being a corporate lawyer is for the most part a constructive endeavor and avoids many of the negative practices that people often complain about concerning lawyers.

Still, being a corporate lawyer is not most people's idea of fun, and the dull, gray nature of much of the work may prove oppressive. Few outsiders will care a whit if you skillfully negotiate a one-dollar increase in the royalty rate for International Buggy Whip, Ltd., in its transglobal licensing deal, even though that may result in a cool extra million in income for the client. Few corporate lawyers get their face plastered over television and become household names. If an in-your-face attitude is what you thrive on, stay out of the corporate field. You were born to litigate.

LITIGATION LAWYERS

Litigation is a whole different ballgame. By the time clients call litigation attorneys, trouble is already brewing. As a result, litigators constantly play catch-up with facts they can't rewrite. Unlike corporate work, where reaching agreement between the two sides is the goal, the ultimate object in litigation is to win. It is as simple as that. There may be plenty of pretrial negotiation back and forth, as the two sides threaten each other with horrible retribution if the suit is not settled. Still, the ultimate goal is to be declared the victor by the judge, while the opposing lawyer sits dejected, trying to figure out what to say to an angry client.

Litigation attorneys immerse themselves in preparation and research. Every angle must be examined, every possible weakness in the other side's case must be probed. What is often frustrating is that hours and hours can be spent looking into some aspect of the case, which may suddenly become moot after a court ruling or a compromise agreement among the parties. While litigation obviously revolves around court cases, a surprisingly large percentage of suits are settled out of court (often at the last possible moment), and so a litigator frequently must spend weeks preparing for a court date that never arrives. The stirring opening statement, rapierlike cross-examinations, and heartfelt summation may wind up in the wastebasket, never used and never appreciated.

Importance of the Courts

A fairly obvious difference between the work of corporate lawyers and litigators is the tremendous importance of the courts. Courts are the powerful third party in the litigation tango. As a litigator, you do not simply deal with the schedules of your side and the other side. You must keep track of when the court will hear the latest motion, or how long it will take for an appeal to be heard. You tend to be active in several courts at once, as you dash from one hearing to another. The courts, in the role of lumbering umpires, serve as referees who must make the call after the two sides fire away at each other with motion after motion. Courts will often set apparently arbitrary deadlines that one side or the other (or both) must scramble to meet.

With courts so important in a litigator's life, it is not enough for a litigator just to understand opposing counsel. Court personnel must be factored into the equation as well. Which judge will hear this case? What sort of arguments will find favor with this judge? Will the judge's clerk let me get away with this motion, or give me a break when a deadline might be missed? How do the rules in this court differ from the rules in the previous court, and how can I use these new rules to my advantage?

Advantages and Disadvantages

A litigator's work life is forever filled with some new brief that must be filed right away or an answer that is due immediately. The issues involved may be complex and unclear, but you *have* to meet that court deadline. Consequently, litigation attorneys frequently must "pull an all-nighter," just as in college or law school, but now with significantly more riding on the work. As a rule, most lawyers tend to work fairly long and hectic days. Litigators work the longest and most hectic of all, and relish it as part of the competitive struggle. They brag about how late they stayed at the office or how long it has been since they took a vacation, implying that they are the only ones in the firm who are really working.

Still, litigation is much more dramatic and exciting than corporate work. There is a special rush of adrenaline that comes whenever you stand up and address the judge or question a witness. Your clients rely on you, not just to help them complete a business deal, but to avoid a harsh verdict from the judge. After all, you may be all that stands between them and some serious fine or jail time. You may love the sense of responsibility and importance this creates, but it also puts added pressure on you. This tends to disturb the sleep of all but the most seasoned litigators.

Two Types of Litigation

The world of litigation can be separated into two distinct hemispheres. On one side is civil litigation, suits by one private party against another. These include claims of breach of contract, misappropriation of company secrets, and personal injury from another person or a product. On the other side is criminal litigation, suits by the government against a private party. These cover charges of murder, robbery, rape, and breaking and entering. Except in some small private law firms that deal with relatively minor matters, any one litigator's practice will rarely involve any significant overlap between civil and criminal cases. This is because the rules for the two types of litigation are quite different, and it is not easy to move back and forth between the two.

Civil Litigation

Civil litigation is somewhat similar to corporate work. Many of the same issues are involved, such as who should be allowed to do what under a contract, and who should bear the economic risk of an enterprise gone bust. In corporate work, however, these issues are more theoretical because they will only apply in case of trouble. In civil litigation there already *is* trouble. Litigators need to interpret language drawn up in happier times to prove that their client is the one who now deserves to get paid for having been wronged.

Civil litigators get a lot of bad press these days over the proliferation of court cases. These are the lawyers who bring million-dollar suits for clients who slip on the ice outside a store or get burnt by hot coffee in a restaurant. They are sometimes labeled ambulance chasers and may appear in intense television commercials that imply that *they* can win you some lotterylike payday, courtesy of the courts. Much of their work is done on a contingency-fee basis, meaning that they get paid only if the client is awarded some money. On the one hand, this system helps poorer clients who could not otherwise afford to seek restitution for a wrong. On the other hand, it encourages lawyers of questionable ethics who might raise specious claims, hoping to become such a nuisance that the defendant will pay money just to make the case go away.

Civil litigation also covers family law, which largely deals with divorce and child custody cases. Divorce lawyers see people at their absolute worst. Even the richest, coolest, most highly educated client can turn into a snarling, vengeful, cruel, and explosive bundle of emotions when going through a divorce and child custody battle. The two sides in divorce actions rarely make decisions based on logic. The high voltage emotions of all involved make the divorce lawyer's job all that much harder. Divorce clients can often try a lawyer's patience, and it takes a real toughness of spirit to handle these types of cases on a regular basis. One of the benefits of working as a divorce lawyer is that you provide much-needed guidance and assistance at a time when the client's whole world seems to be crashing down. In these situations, the litigator truly earns the title of counselor. If you win, you have your client's undying admiration (except for that huge bill, of course). If you lose, well, divorce clients rarely turn into repeat business anyway.

Criminal Litigation

In criminal litigation you leave the niceties of the business world behind and deal with the darker instincts of the human animal. Private criminal litigators are, by definition, defense attorneys, since the state always handles the role of prosecution. While a criminal case may involve defendants that are corporations, criminal litigation usually involves individuals, who tend to be much tougher characters than clients in civil cases. The client in a criminal defense case who has been in and out of trouble with the police all his life may not relate well to a lawyer who spent nineteen years in school, and vice versa.

Our legal system is based on the theory that even the most heinous mass murderer deserves a vigorous defense. It is the state that must prove the accused guilty. "All" the defense must do to obtain an acquittal is convince a jury that the state has not done its job of prosecution well enough. Still, criminal defense lawyers, even the high-priced ones who represent celebrities or organized crime bosses, face a tough task. The government is always a formidable opponent, with a myriad of ways of using its extensive powers to push for a conviction. Defending someone accused of a crime may require deep digging into the legal bag of tricks, in order to construct legal roadblocks designed to keep some of the state's evidence from being presented.

Criminal defense work can be intensely challenging, but it can present a most difficult problem. At times, a criminal defense lawyer must figure out what to do when faced with the (confidential) knowledge that the client is actually guilty of the crime he or she is being tried for. In this situation, it is still the defense counsel's job to explore every possible weakness in the state's case and to search for some possible reason (such as insanity) why the state should not mete out punishment. It is the lawyer's role to keep personal conclusions private and to professionally use all of the safeguards built into our system to protect the client from a rush to judgment. It is the role of the judge and jury to decide who is guilty and what penalties should be handed out.

OTHER SUB-SPECIALTIES

While corporate and litigation work are the best-known categories of private law practice, there are many other sub-specialties that deserve mention:

- real estate
- tax

- labor
- environmental law
- patents
- immigration

Real Estate

These lawyers spend much of their time assisting in the sale and purchase of land. They are also heavily involved in negotiating leases, land development, zoning battles, environmental regulation, and simple business loans. Real estate work can range from helping your neighbors down the street sell their home to assisting a real estate empire diversify its holdings in a distant part of the state.

Tax

Lawyers specializing in tax are involved in almost every aspect of civil law, as virtually every action has a tax effect. Tax lawyers, who are often also accountants, are indispensable for planning corporate transactions. Their responsibilities spill over into litigation, as they handle suits brought by or against the Internal Revenue Service or other taxing authorities who seek a larger chunk of the client's cash. To work in the tax field, you must become intimate with the Internal Revenue Code, a highly convoluted document that governs the American tax system. Beyond that, you must be able to handle volumes and volumes of IRS regulations and private IRS rulings that deal with the fine points of interpretation of the tax law.

Labor

At its most basic, labor law involves working on employment contracts, but it also covers discrimination claims and cases of fired workers. Labor lawyers tend to receive their greatest public attention when they are involved in the frequently complex world of union representation and collective bargaining agreements. A lawyer who specializes in labor issues usually represents either management or labor; only a few cross back and forth between the two sides. The central aspect of labor law is that employment issues cut right to the heart of people's economic life, and the negotiations and the emotions can be heated.

Environmental Law

This is a fairly new specialty in the legal world, as most of the rules governing the environment are less than twenty-five years old. This is a mere blink of the eye compared to the centuries-old tradition of real estate law. To truly understand environmental law, a basic knowledge of engineering and science will come in handy, as technical issues abound in this field. Environmental law involves yet another series of ultra-detailed regulations that few outsiders dare to peruse. The split in this group is between those who push to expand the control government exerts over the environment and those who seek to ease the rules businesses must follow to comply with the latest environmental requirement. The two sides view themselves, respectively, as those who are truly doing their fellow citizens a service by cleaning our planet and those who are trying to help struggling companies deal rationally with an often scattershot and wasteful series of rules.

Patents

Patent lawyers also tend to have a scientific slant, as they must be able to converse intelligently about inventions that are on the cutting edge of technology. They work with inventors (solo or within a company) who have developed new products or new ways of performing a task. When inventors apply for a patent, they ask the government to certify that they own the innovation and may reap the profit from its use. Obtaining a patent can take years, because the government responds very slowly and deliberately to new applications. The patent application process is so complicated that few inventors can handle it alone without the help of a legal specialist. Great persistence is needed, and patent lawyers must often deal with anxious clients who cannot understand what is taking so long.

Immigration

By definition, immigration attorneys have a highly cosmopolitan clientele that can make for a nice, steady stream of business. They deal with everything from a foreign student trying to avoid deportation after a run-in with the local constables during a beer bash, to a highly paid multinational corporate executive trying to receive permission to move his family to the United States for a short sabbatical. Proficiency in several languages, of course, is almost a requirement in this area.

WHERE WILL YOU WIND UP?

At this point in your life, you are probably having enough trouble trying to decide whether to go to law school and, if so, which schools to apply to. Few prospective law students can really decide on their future specialty before the first day of law school. Exposure to different types of law courses usually helps steer students toward the areas they prefer.

Sometimes, the ultimate decision on a specialty is determined by the simple luck of the draw, where the staffing needs of your first employer determine where you begin your legal specialization. If you definitely prefer one area of law over another (or you definitely do not want to get into one particular area), you will need to make this clear at job interview time, and you will need to do extra homework when scouting out prospective employers. Hopefully, you will be in a position to have some say in what you wind up doing in the profession of law. However, when the legal job market is tight, many new graduates do not have that luxury.

PART TWO

PREPARING FOR LAW SCHOOL

8

MAKING THE MOST
OUT OF COLLEGE

Deciding you want to go to law school is a difficult mental task. Going ahead and preparing for law school is more of an organizational dilemma. The process can last a year or two, or more, depending on your personal situation. Part Two of the book covers the time period between when you decide to go to law school and when you finally begin the application process. For some of you this period may only last two or three days. For example, if you have already graduated from college, then you can start sending for applications right away, and these two chapters will not have much significance for you. However, if you are still an undergraduate, or if you have not yet even begun your college career, there is a lot of time left before you begin the law school application process. You still have time to mold your college career in ways that can affect your future plans for law school.

ACADEMICS

The two most important factors in determining your chances of being accepted at the law school of your choice are your college grade-point average (GPA) and your score on the Law School Admission Test (LSAT). Taking the LSAT is usually a one-shot event, and while there are many things you can do to prepare in advance of the test (see Chapter 13), the preparation is limited to a few months beforehand. There is not much you can do years in advance that will specifically help your

LSAT score, but your college GPA *is* something that you can work on during your entire tenure as an undergraduate.

Naturally, if you have already graduated from college, your GPA is a given. It is carved in stone in your transcript, and you must deal with it as is, for better or worse. If you are still toiling away as an undergraduate, your GPA fate has yet to be sealed, and you still have a chance to help yourself in this area. Seniors, and to an extent juniors, have only limited maneuvering room. A fantastic year of straight A's will only help to a limited extent when averaged with three years of C's. Those who are freshmen or sophomores, and especially those who have not even started college still have time to improve their chances of being accepted into law school.

Of course, your GPA is not the only fact about your college career that is important in terms of getting into law school. Where you go to college is also vital. Coming in tenth in your class at Harvard will mean far more to law school admissions officials than coming in third at Podunk U. Getting into a good college depends on factors such as your high school grades and your financial resources, and this topic is really beyond the scope of this book. Clearly, attending a good college will help you, no matter what you do after you graduate. Equally obvious is that whatever college you attend, you should try to get good grades. You don't need us to tell you that. Still, you should not try to artificially inflate your college grades by taking mostly easy courses, as this is not going to help you either in the short or the long term. Law school admissions officers see your entire transcript, not just your GPA, so you will not get much mileage out of straight A's in Remedial Basket Weaving and Rock 'n' Roll—The Disco Years. What's more, taking easy courses wastes your invaluable college years. The real point of college is to learn things that can be useful to you in the future and turn you into an adult with a well-rounded education.

CHOOSING A COLLEGE MAJOR

"Fine," you say, "I'll take challenging courses in college, but what should I take that will help me in law school and later on as an attorney?" The lawyerly answer is that there *is* no simple answer to that question. Unlike some professional schools (such as medical schools), law schools do not have any college prerequisite courses. Applicants can have majored in anything at all in their undergraduate days. Majoring either in a formal pre-law program or in something apparently far removed from law such as biology will not by itself either help or hinder your chances for law school acceptance. Law schools are looking for applicants who can demonstrate intellectual skills, not those who have substantive knowledge of particular topics. Because of this, and because the basic natures of college and law school are so different, there is usually little correlation between what classes you take in college and the classes you will take in law school.

The dissimilarity between college and law school revolves around the different ways you are required to think. As a gross simplification, college is a continuation of the basic high school teaching method of the teacher dispensing wisdom and the students gathering up the knowledge and spewing it back at the professor when required. At its core, law school forces the students to figure out on their own the significance of the material studied, with a premium placed on organized and cogent thinking. Thus, any college course that develops your ability to think clearly and independently will benefit you in law school and when practicing law. The only specific skill that you really need to develop in preparation for law school is the ability to write with clarity and precision. A lawyer's work usually involves significant amounts of writing, and the careful use of words is one of a lawyer's chief weapons. The more your writing abilities can be honed as an undergraduate, the better off you will be when it comes time for those writing-intensive law exams.

Political Science and History, the Most Common Majors for Law Students

If you walk around a law firm and ask the attorneys what their majors were in college, you may receive a fairly uniform response. Traditionally, majoring in political science or history has been the typical path to law school, and these are still the most common college majors for new lawyers. This may be changing, though; these days you will also find a good representation from other disciplines, such as languages, philosophy, and even the sciences.

It is not hard to see why political science and history have long been the common denominators among many proto-law students. Both topics focus, to a large extent, on how governments work and how people interact with authority. Those are the core issues lawyers deal with on a daily basis, so it is not much of a stretch to move from studying history and politics to studying law. Politics is the debate over how people should act and how society uses force, in varying degrees, to make people act that way. History is largely the study of political debates in former eras. Law is the process where there is a clash of interests between people, and the government settles the dispute by enforcing the rules of society (the rules established through the process of politics). It sounds so simple and circular.

There is no question that political science and history classes can prove useful in law school. If nothing else, these classes help explain the general structure of government, but chances are you learned most of the real basics in high school. Majoring in either political science or history will further expand your knowledge of government and is a perfectly fine choice for the lawyer-to-be. We both took this path through college (Chris majored in European history and Harry in political science), even though neither of us had yet decided to go on to law school. While few of our college major courses directly prepared us for law school, Harry was greatly helped by taking business law as part of his political science course requirements. That course provided a wonderful introduction to common legal topics (such as contracts, business organizations, and court procedures) that helped Harry better understand the subjects covered in his first-year law school classes.

Other Majors

Once you get away from the traditional political science/history axis, you will find that many college majors also provide valuable tools you can use later in the field of law. Virtually any major has redeeming value, but we see particular benefit in:

- mathematics and other sciences
- philosophy
- economics
- anthropology

- psychology
- religion
- languages

Mathematics and Other Sciences

These subjects are perfectly reasonable majors for pre-law students. With their emphasis on exactitude and finding the correct answers, these disciplines help sharpen a student's mind, and they can be helpful when later performing legal tasks such as separating the truly important issues from the surface trappings. The sciences heavily rely on research, which is the same as in the legal field. The only problem is that, unlike in the sciences, law is hardly ever a black-and-white arena. The myriad of nuances in legal issues that can cloud a result will infuriate the mathematician, who simply wants to deduce the correct answer.

Analytical Philosophy

This subject involves the never-ending analysis of arcane and apparently inconsequential items of thought, making it an ideal study for lawyers-to-be. No idea is safe from attack, and you must always be ready to defend your core concepts. This style of thinking fits easily into the mode used in law school. Each idea espoused will be picked over and scrutinized, either by the law professor or your fellow law students. Argument for argument's sake often seems to be the goal in both philosophy and law school, in that arguments help you sharpen your ability to defend an intellectual position. A shortcoming of the philosophy major turned lawyer is that he or she can get lost in mental gymnastics and lose sight of the fact that, as a practicing lawyer, you must actually come to a conclusion and *do* something.

Economics

You really should explore this topic at least once while in college, especially if you plan on going into corporate law. Knowing the basic terminology of the world of finance will be extraordinarily valuable in the days to come, even if you have no plans to become a business tycoon yourself. When dealing with the business world, you will need to understand at least a modicum of what business clients are telling you, and they will likely be speaking the language of economics and finance, not the language of law. It's *your* job to understand them, not vice versa.

Other majors may prove somewhat less directly beneficial to a law career.

Anthropology or Psychology

Any study of the way people behave provides a base of knowledge concerning the human thought process. This will prove highly useful in law, when you need to grasp the hidden intentions of those on the other side of a case *and* of your own client.

Religion

Religion has been the source of many of the central ideals and theories that drive large segments of society. Thus, the study of this subject also sheds light on the human condition and prepares future lawyers for dealing with a wide range of people.

Foreign Languages

Language courses can help you understand some of the esoteric and foreign-originating terms that appear in law and provide a decided advantage if you intend to specialize in international or immigration law.

College is important in and of itself, and even the most eager prospective lawyer should not view it as simply a means of getting into law school. If you acquire a well-rounded education at a respectable college and earn good grades in courses that sharpen your thinking while developing your writing skills, you will have done almost everything you can to make the most of your college career.

FORGING RELATIONSHIPS WITH PROFESSORS

College also provides you with an opportunity to cultivate relationships with professors, which can further assist you in your long-range goal of getting into law school. These relationships may come in the form of working together on an independent study project, assisting professors in their research, or simply discussing class topics during office hours or at informal get-togethers. A close relationship with professors has both a general dividend not related to law school and one that *is* pertinent to your future plans. Getting to know your professors outside of the formal classroom setting can expose you to insights and learning that transcends the four corners of your course syllabus. In an informal setting, professors can provide a great link between the somewhat sheltered academic world and the vast expanse of life after graduation. This can open your eyes to knowledge of the outside world as well as introduce you to applications of your learning that you may not have considered.

Aside from this general benefit, your professors can also serve as an ideal source of recommendations for your law school application. College professors have a unique and timely insight into your learning abilities, your intellectual maturity, and your growth potential. These are all topics that carry a lot of weight with law school admissions offices, faced with many applicants with similar GPAs and LSAT scores. Keep in mind that a recommendation from at least one college professor is required by most law schools in their application process, unless you have been out of college for some years.

Professors can also act as something of an unofficial guidance counselor to students considering law school. They may have a sense for whether your intellectual style is suited for law, and they may offer some tips on which law schools are worth considering or avoiding. Their opinions may not be all that scientific, but chances are the opinions of your professors will be as relatively unbiased as those of any other adults you are likely to encounter during college.

COLLEGE GUIDANCE COUNSELORS

On a more formal basis, most colleges have professional guidance counselors who can serve as a ready source of information and material to help you decide whether to apply to law school (and if so, where). They can save you considerable hassle and time, and if they do not have the material you want, they may at least tell you where to find it.

Because of their formal status, college guidance counselors may be more reluctant than professors to give you firm opinions about what schools might be good for you. A counselor will probably stick to the "well, on this hand . . . and on the other hand . . ." style of recommendation, and you should not get upset if this is the limit of what they will tell you. In the end, the decision of whether to go to law school, and if so, where, rests with you. A counselor can point you in the right direction, but you must synthesize the information and make up your own mind.

EXTRACURRICULAR ACTIVITIES

College is not all academics, and your GPA, course transcript, and academic recommendations are not the sum total of your college record that will appear in your law school application. To be honest, those three items *are* the key elements of college that determine your chances for admission to law school. Still, your college extracurricular activities can have an effect on your life in the law. Frankly, this effect may be felt far more once you get into law school (and during your later legal career) than in the short-range process of trying to get *into* law school. Serving as president of your college debate team or working as a stringer for a national news wire service will probably not make many law school admissions officers stop what they are doing to mark you as accepted on the spot. However, both of those activities (and many others) can truly help prepare you for law school and the law in ways that no classroom experience can.

Just as there is no mandatory major for prospective law students, there is no set extracurricular activity that tomorrow's law students should not miss. While almost any kind of college extracurricular activity will help develop some social or intellectual skills, the activities that will prove helpful in a law setting are those that require you to develop skills used by law students and by lawyers. Examples of these types of activities include:

- journalism
- debating
- student government
- public interest groups
- athletics
- drama

Journalism

The worlds of journalism and law are quite distinct, but there can be significant overlap between them in terms of skills. Working on the college newspaper or radio station will get you used to meeting unforgiving deadlines that you simply cannot avoid and dealing with late-breaking developments that nobody expected. What better way to get ready for being a young associate at a law firm? If you have coped with trashing your laid-out copy for the next day's newspaper in order to make room for coverage of the firing of a local controversial professor, you will not be shocked by having to rewrite an entire brief when the judge in your case issues some unexpected ruling. Harry spent most of his undergraduate free time working at the college radio station. After getting used to producing a thirty-minute weekly public affairs documentary show that *had* to be ready to air at 6:00 P.M. Friday, Harry did not become overly rattled when, years later, a client informed him that the latest draft of the new contract *had* to be ready by the end of the day.

Journalism, if taught properly, emphasizes the ability to organize your thoughts and to express them cogently and precisely. These are exactly the same traits that law schools seek to develop. If you can begin law school with the ability to write and think clearly, you will have a decided advantage over more than half of your classmates.

Classic journalism also emphasizes impartiality. Reporters are supposed to be able to see both sides of the story and report them fairly. Law students and lawyers must also see beyond their own prejudices and conclusions to understand the strengths and weaknesses of both sides. If you have experience in writing newspaper articles that include fair discussions of positions with which you strongly disagree, you will not be at a loss when you need to convince a judge or jury of the merits of your client's position, which you privately believe to be highly questionable.

Working on the campus newspaper or radio station also serves as an effective way for you to get to know the powerful players in the university cosmos, and that can provide some direct help in getting into law school. If you wind up making a favorable impression on any of the local movers and shakers, they can be valuable sources of recommendations when it comes time to submit law school applications.

Debating

Debating teams are not as common on campus as they were one and two generations ago, but the formalistic and intellectual exploits of debating are perfect preparations for the law. Haggling with fellow debaters over seemingly innocuous minutiae will prepare you for equally obscure discussions with your law school colleagues. Given the similarities in how debate teams and lawyers operate, don't be surprised to find many of your debate teammates following you right along to law school.

More important, on a debate team, you are assigned a position on an issue (which may well be a position you oppose) and you must defend it. You research your issue, scouting out arguments that support your side, and then you must prepare a well-organized and persuasive defense of your position. Guess what? That is precisely what lawyers do in preparing for a case. You may not believe in or support your client's position, but it is your job to gather and present all the facts you can muster to defend that stance.

Harry recalls an experience in a college public speaking class, when the assignment was to prepare a short talk on why Richard Nixon should be remembered as one of America's finest presidents. At the time (the mid-1970s), few if any students in the class believed that was true, and most could not suspend their own beliefs and view the issue from another angle. While he was equally anti-Nixon, Harry saw the assignment as an interesting intellectual experiment and was able to draft a rational argument in favor of Nixon. In the years to come, Harry often recalled that lesson when performing very similar mental gymnastics in order to draft arguments in favor of a client's position.

Student Government/Public Interest Groups

Involvement with student government in college will provide you with a modicum of exposure to how political groups operate. However, the usual lack of authority in student government robs the experience of much real significance. You can achieve more valuable experience by becoming involved in some form of public interest group on campus; these groups usually have far more clear-cut agendas than student government. Seeking to implement far-reaching goals through an interest group also teaches you how differing segments of the population seek to have their positions adopted by society as a whole, which is a process similar to that of making laws.

Athletics

Considering the highly cerebral nature of law, it may seem incongruous, but college athletics can also be a great way to prepare for practicing law. Most athletic competition serves as a wonderful way to learn to work within a hierarchical organization, where everyone needs to pull together for the good of the team. That kind of training can help you in almost any sort of business endeavor, not just law. More specifically, athletics develops determination, persistence, and the ability to perform under pressure. These are traits sorely needed in both law school and in practicing law. As noted in Chapter 1, litigation attorneys frequently have athletics in their backgrounds, as the competitive drive and zeal needed for waging legal combat mirrors that required on the playing field.

Drama

In Chapter 1 we also noted that the flip side of the litigation personality is the theatrical bent. While a majority of theater majors do not usually wind up at law school, participating in some extracurricular theatrical activities in college can be a great help for tomorrow's courtroom star. If you can come into law school having lost the fear of public speaking that grips so many students, you will have an advantage when it comes time to pontificate in class or prepare for moot court arguments. Later, when you need to get up in a crowded courtroom and address an audience of one (the judge), having experience in performing before tough audiences can only be a plus.

How Extracurricular Activities Might Help You Get into Law School

Simply participating in any of these extracurricular activities will probably make little difference in your chances for acceptance at the law school of your choice. The vast majority of applicants will have engaged in some sort of activity outside of class in college. You will not be the only one stating that you learned ever so much about life by working at the *State U Daily Herald*. One of the few aspects of extracurricular activities that has a realistic chance of making any sort of impression on the law school admissions office is if you report you filled some serious leadership slots in your chosen field. The difference between saying you worked on the school newspaper and stating that you were the student editor of the paper is huge. Leadership roles, by definition, make you stand out from the rest. Leadership roles show that others in authority saw enough talent and skill in you to put their faith in your ability to lead others and get things done. In effect, this is another form of recommendation, one that often speaks much louder than some self-serving words scribbled on a piece of paper.

Leadership roles are good for you for two reasons. The first is that, yes, they will help you get into law school. The second is that they simply benefit your inner growth. Attaining leadership roles develops your self-confidence and your ability to organize others. If you are secure in your ability to handle public responsibilities, you will be much less likely to fall prey to the gnawing self-doubts that can ruin even the smartest student's first year of law school. Later, you will be better suited to handle the pressure of solving very personal and important issues for your clients.

If you are organized enough to be in the position of getting ready for law school before you near the end of your college career, the tips in this chapter can hopefully provide some guidance about how to best spend your undergraduate days. College is too important a part of your education to waste it simply in preparing to apply to law school. The key thing is to try to bring some sense of organization to your college actions. No matter what you plan to do once you graduate from college, you need to concentrate on what college classes and activities will help you in one form or another in the future and try to avoid things that do nothing to help your growth as an educated person. If, upon careful consideration, some of the things you decide to do in college wind up helping you later in law school or in the law, all the better. If they have absolutely no effect on your legal career at all, but they taught you something important or developed some important skill, then they were worth it.

9

WHEN TO GO
TO LAW SCHOOL

In the entire process of preparing for law school, the hardest question by far is whether to go to law school at all. Once you overcome that hurdle, the second most difficult question is where to apply to law school (which we discuss in Chapters 10–12). Between these two paramount issues is a third topic that, while of lesser impact, deserves serious consideration: when should you go to law school?

The issue of deciding when to apply to law school has practical import only for those still in college. If you are already out of college and have decided on law school, chances are the time to apply is as soon as possible. Of course, people in this position still must consider the actual mechanics of applying, such as deciding when to apply for the Law School Admission Test (LSAT) and when to send in applications. Still, these are timing issues that all applicants must address. However, those of you still in college must consider a timing issue somewhat unique to your status: Is it better to apply during senior year in order to begin law school in the fall after college graduation, or wait one or two years or even more and do something else before embarking on the law school process?

TO WAIT OR NOT TO WAIT?—THE
ADVANTAGES OF WAITING

Our answer is a resounding "wait!" Naturally, everyone in this situation must make up his or her own mind, and there are many people who go directly from college to law school without suffering any form of serious trauma. Still, we sincerely believe that most people will be far readier for law school and, what is more important, will obtain a far greater benefit from law school if they allow more than just another summer vacation to come between college and law school. Both of us waited. Chris did not begin law school for two years after college, and Harry waited a full five years before returning to school.

Why wait? For one thing, after sixteen straight years of formal schooling, it will do you a world of good to give yourself a break from the classroom routine. Law school is a highly intense experience, especially in the first year. It's likely to be the toughest academic experience you will ever face, and if you do not take some time off, you are far more likely to suffer from schooling burnout and give in to the high level of stress in law school. After being away from a school setting for a while, returning may almost feel nostalgic. Time away from the classroom may make you far more willing to get back into the routine of homework, teachers, and tests.

Added Maturity

More important, as mentioned in Chapter 2, law school is a very different sort of educational experience than college, and a little extra life experience can better prepare you for it. The independent, logical, concise thinking required in law school is, quite frankly, often lacking in the mind of the average twenty-two-year-old who has done hardly anything in life but go to school. The extra time and responsibility of being on your own for a while can add a great deal to the maturity of a student.

If you insist on looking at the issue in purely goal-oriented terms, just think of taking time off as a great way to get an advantage over some of your younger, less sophisticated classmates. In addition, having some nonschool experience on your resume is a plus when trying to make yourself stand out for law school admissions purposes. Taking time off between college and law school is now a well-established practice followed by many lawyers, so your carrying on of that tradition should not be seen as a negative by future potential employers.

More Practical Experience

One of the primary benefits in taking time off is acquiring more practical experience in the world. Many students hold summer jobs from the teen years on. Some even hold demanding part-time jobs through high school and college. These experiences are all valid and useful, but they cannot compare to the value of spending your full time doing something else besides attending school. Anything you do full time (other than schooling) brings you into contact with people who are dealing with problems more complex than those faced by most students. This exposure to nonschool life will help when you get back to class in law school. The curriculum in law school is highly theoretical and impractical. If your life consists almost exclusively of classroom experiences, you can easily get caught up in the imposing intellectual facade of law school topics. If, on the other hand, you have solid experience dealing with people in many walks of life and the problems they face, you can more readily see behind the superstructure of law school discussions. The extra maturity may allow you to better grasp the practical impact and meaning that, in most cases, lie behind even the most impenetrable legal theory. To put it more simply, it is usually the students right out of college who get caught up in the stereotypical picayune first-year-law-school arguments over largely meaningless nuances in the law. Those who have been out for a while are more concerned with grasping the essential message of the lesson and tend not to sweat the small stuff.

Standing Out from the Crowd

Taking time off can improve your appreciation of and performance in law school, but it can also help you avoid the worst mistake you can make in this area. There is nothing worse than going to law school after college just because you can't think of anything else to do or just because all your friends are going. Attending law school is simply too expensive, time-consuming, and important for that type of lazy decision making. The time and experience away from college help you make a more thoughtful and rational decision about whether law school is right for you. If you try doing something else for a while or at least remove yourself from the lockstep world of higher education, your decision will be more voluntary and thus better suited for you.

WHAT TO DO BETWEEN COLLEGE AND LAW SCHOOL

So, if you do take time off after college graduation, what should you do? The best answer is, get a job. Almost any job will do, as long as you find it interesting, it's full time, and you earn enough to make ends meet. If eventually you do go to law school, you will bring with you a storehouse of practical life experiences that will make it easier for you to relate to many issues that arise while studying law. If nothing else, your time in the work force will prove a valuable lesson in how to interact with people in the business world and how to conduct yourself in a professional setting. This may not do much for you in law school, but you will appreciate its value three years later when you begin your legal career.

Work

During your time off, you may wish to get as far away from the legal field as possible, to see if some other line of work catches your fancy. Act as if you don't intend to go to law school, and aim for an entry-level position in another field you are considering for your career. For example, try landing a job at your local newspaper, apply for jobs in a nearby government agency, try retail sales, try working in the family business, or even try starting your own business. If you wind up loving your job and thriving, great, maybe you can forget all about law school. If you wind up unsatisfied or unexcited about working your way up in that environment, and law school still appeals to you, then maybe you *should* apply.

Another approach is to get as close to the world of law as you can, to get a better sense of whether it appeals to you. The best choice you can make in this scenario is to serve as a paralegal at a local law firm. Paralegals are nonlawyers who assist lawyers by performing tasks (such as filling out forms, organizing documents, or even doing some research) that really do not require a legal education and are not usually worth a lawyer's hourly rate. Paralegals work closely with attorneys and get an intimate look at what it means to be a lawyer. Most paralegals know more about the practical aspects of lawyering than almost anyone else starting law school, not to mention most first-year associates.

Even a nonlaw job in a law firm, such as messenger, secretary, or receptionist, can allow you to see the inner workings of the firm. As a side benefit, any type of work at a law firm will allow you to knowingly toss around some legal terms, such as *subpoenas, interrogatories,* and *appellate briefs,* that will impress your classmates when (and if) you do start law school.

After spending time working at a law firm, you may find the legal setting exciting and challenging and want to become a real player in that process. If so, you've waited long enough; it's time to sign up for the LSAT and send for law school applications. However, direct exposure to the legal world may lead you to conclude that the life of a lawyer is not at all what you had imagined and that law school is not for you. If so, you have just saved yourself thousands of dollars in tuition bills and three years of hard struggle. You can now freely go on to do something else with your life.

For those of you who are absolutely, positively confident that law school is in your future, working for a year or so can still be a plus. You can take a middle-of-the-road approach by working at a job that has law connections but focuses on the world outside a law firm. Try working as an aide to your congressperson or state legislator, to experience the law-making process firsthand. If you do not have the necessary political connections for that sort of job, try any of the numerous groups that help people in trouble, such as welfare rights groups, a charity, or a government agency. This will get you used to dealing with people who need help resolving important personal problems. After all, that is exactly what most lawyers do most of the time.

We both worked in Washington, D.C., between college and law school—Chris at the U.S. Department of Health and Human Services, and Harry at the Democratic National Committee. Interestingly enough, we had each decided at the end of college that we did *not* want to go to law school, but we both began to change our minds by the end of our time in Washington. For the most part, this change of heart was due to our exposure to people who *had* gone to law school and had survived to lead interesting lives.

Earn Another Degree

Working is often the best thing you can do between college and law school, but there are other options that may be better suited to your temperament, intellectual interests, and financial situation. One alternative is to earn a different professional degree. This option is sometimes a default process, in that you may head right to medical school after college, only to suddenly realize you simply cannot stand the sight of blood. At that point (hopefully before you have sent in too many tuition payments), law school might start looking far more appealing than it did before. A more common approach to the multiple-degree option is to try to blend two different disciplines. For example, you may first earn a graduate degree in engineering and *then* earn your law degree, so that you can combine your educational credentials in order to specialize in an area you love. In this way, you could either aim for a legal job involving engineering matters, or you could work directly in engineering with the added bonus of a solid knowledge of the legal aspects of that field. In either event, your multiple degrees will give you a decided advantage and added marketability over those with just one degree.

The most popular example of this double-degree scenario is the combination M.B.A. (Master of Business Administration) and J.D. degree. This powerful combination can open many doors for new job seekers. Business executives frequently need attorneys to explain the legal ramifications of their actions, and lawyers frequently feel limited by a lack of knowledge of how to translate their advice into practical action by a business client. If the business executive already knows the basics of how the law works, or if the lawyer has a thorough grasp of how businesses operate, they can operate more self-sufficiently in their field. In the best possible combination, you might work for a year or two in a business that appeals to you, then earn your M.B.A. followed by a J.D. degree. You will then have as well-rounded a background as is humanly possible for dealing with the legal aspects of business problems once your schooling is over. The only problem is that this plan eats up more time and money than many are willing to invest.

One way to shorten the length of time needed to earn a double degree is to participate in a joint degree program (discussed in Chapter 4). By combining the school work needed for these degrees, universities offering joint degree programs allow you to complete the requirements for the multiple degrees in less time (and for less tuition) than if you earned the degrees separately. Handling the combination workload is not easy, but considering the savings in time and money, this is a wonderful opportunity for those who are certain of their chosen aspect of law.

The real drawback of earning another degree before your J.D. is that it is just more schooling. It does not provide the mental break or the refreshing splash of reality that comes from leaving the books behind and beginning to interact with the outside world. The number of people able to properly plan, execute, and pay for an almost decade-long process of working and then earning multiple degrees is decidedly small.

Travel

For those considering law school, the time between college and law school may well be the last chance for truly unfettered, irresponsible, extended fun and adventure for *many* years. If you are old enough to be able to live on your own and earn enough to live on, but young enough not to be encumbered by the web of responsibilities that comes with maturity (a spouse, children, a mortgage, etc.), you have a golden opportunity. After all, law school lasts a very long three years. After law school, the economic pressure of debt incurred for schooling usually demands that you start work immediately. Once you start working, well . . . the next thing you know forty years have sped by, someone's throwing you a retirement party, and you are more interested in quality health care than in backpacking through Bulgaria.

If you can swing it, take some time between college and law school to travel. Take six months or a year, and visit the place of your dreams. It could be to the big city downstate or halfway around the world, or it could be one long trip to a whole slew of exotic locales. Chris spent a full year studying and traveling in India on a Rotary scholarship, and Harry spent several months traveling on his own across the United States while between jobs. For both of us, this time far from home opened our eyes to new ways of thinking and remains part of our fondest memories.

It's not as if extended travel is a totally decadent idea. You *can* do something else besides sightseeing and trying to date the alluring natives. You can pick up some sort of job, whether or not you really need the salary. Working while you travel provides you with several benefits at once. Working in your new locale adds to your real-world experience that can help so much in law school. Meanwhile, the travel aspect will expose you to different people and cultures, providing you with a greater understanding of the human condition, a quality needed by virtually all lawyers. On top of all that, a description of your exciting exploits can even help spice up your law school application.

Once you head off to law school and then land a full-time job, your life in the law will probably contain more than your fill of regiment, drudgery, and responsibility. To be fair, this is true of most professions. The frequent dullness of adult life is far easier to accept if you can at least look back with a warm glow on the year or so in your mid-twenties when you were mostly carefree and on your own. You may not have the chance for that kind of freedom again for another forty years (if at all), so give yourself a break and go have fun.

Then go to law school.

PART THREE

APPLYING AND DECIDING

10

THINKING ABOUT
LAW SCHOOLS

The momentous decision to apply to law school is quickly followed by a simple but daunting question. Where? Choosing schools that will receive the benefit of your application (and application fee) is a difficult decision. There are hundreds of schools, each with its own characteristics, programs, and reputations, which are virtually impossible to quantify. Faced with this wide array, you can wind up wrestling with long lists of qualities, trying to balance apples and oranges. Does a larger library compensate for poor living accommodations? Does a better academic reputation justify living in the middle of urban blight for three years? Our answers to these questions are, respectively, "not even close" and "probably," but you might feel quite differently.

This does not mean that there is a shortage of authorities who claim to know what the answers are. Books, advisers, and "knowledgeable" relatives abound, each prescribing what schools are best for you. While these sources can be invaluable, always remember one caveat to any advice you receive: pay attention to your gut instincts. The comparisons you will be making are so subjective that no one else can fully reflect your personal taste. You are the one who will have to live with your decision. Do your own research, make your own evaluations, and then go with the options that just seem right to you.

You need to impose some order on this unwieldy balancing test. Haphazard investigations are approximately as useful as holding a seance to decide where to apply. Our suggestion is to condense the entire gamut of choices into three essential questions:

- Which law schools are best for you?
- Which law schools might accept you?
- Which law schools can you afford?

This chapter suggests ways for you to determine the answer to the first question, and Chapters 11 and 12 discuss the last two.

WHICH LAW SCHOOLS ARE BEST FOR YOU?

It makes a lot of sense for you to compile a wish list of ideal law schools before you pare it down on the basis of cost or chances of admission. Doing so helps clarify what you rather than some book feel are the most important qualities in a law school. Realistically, you will focus on schools within a certain range of competitiveness when you look at these qualities, but try to investigate schools you might think a bit above you and a bit below you in order to extend the range of possibilities. A simple chart for comparisons, including the schools, your impressions, and the factors that you consider the most important, can be a great help in organizing your thoughts.

There are too many statistics and aspects concerning law schools to consider all of them equally. You must determine what is most important to you to make your investigation of law schools effective. This chapter will help you rank the schools that interest you, but remember this: any attempt to rank the importance of the characteristics you analyze is as subjective as the efforts to rank the schools themselves. You might feel the single most important criterion is the presence of courses on Eskimo law. This makes you different, but if there is a rational reason for your preference (perhaps you foresee a thriving practice in a sub-specialty that has not attracted a glut of lawyers), then adjust your own list accordingly.

The typical person will want a more balanced approach to evaluating law schools. One good way to organize the myriad characteristics of law schools is to divide them into two broad categories:

- those that have a direct impact upon your job prospects when you graduate
- those that have a direct impact on your quality of life during law school

Most people put more emphasis on the first set of factors, since getting a job is the primary reason that most people attend law school. It is an undeniable fact that the graduates of some schools are better placed than others to get blue-chip, or even any, jobs. If you do well in law school, you will get a job. The difference between the most favorably regarded school and the least is that the definition of doing well changes. Passing may be enough at top schools, whereas only the very top scholars at a less competitive place may have excellent job prospects.

On the other hand, do not ignore the second set of factors. You should think hard before sacrificing quality-of-life issues in exchange for the nebulous idea that one school is generally more favored by employers. On purely pragmatic grounds, if you do well at a less prestigious school, you will be as, if not more, attractive to prospective employers than if you do poorly at a prestigious one. On a personal level, law school will consume at least three years of your life. A small sacrifice in name recognition may add inestimably to your enjoyment of those three years. In turn, this will have a direct effect upon your chances of academic success. The contribution of a nice, affordable apartment in a safe neighborhood to your grades is intangible but quite real. Finally, the quality-of-life factors may also have indirect but important effects on your job prospects. For example, a school with a large class size translates into more graduates, which translates into a larger alumni network, which may translate into a better chance of a job if you meet one of these industrious alumni.

Our experience supports the importance of the quality-of-life factors. Harry was drawn to the idea of going to school in Boston, where he grew up, and the proximity to his family added greatly to his law school experience. Meanwhile, Chris met many people at Harvard who had chosen the school solely because of its reputation and then came to doubt that they had made the correct decision. Some of them would undoubtedly have been better off in a more familiar location, possibly at a less prestigious institution.

Characteristics That Affect Your Job Prospects

Accreditation

You must pass the bar to get virtually any job in law. One prerequisite to taking the bar in almost every state is a degree from a law school that the American Bar Association has accredited. Accordingly, you should ensure that all schools you consider are accredited. A majority of institutions have passed this test, but there are a few that have not. Nonaccredited schools are either quite new or located in states that do not require a degree from an accredited school to pass the bar (most notably California). They tend to be cheaper, have an older group of students, allow their students to keep another full-time job, and have lower admission standards. These advantages are almost completely offset by the strict limits the lack of accreditation imposes on the school's graduates, because the degree is worth little in most states. You should think hard about your job prospects and career plans when you consider nonaccredited schools.

Reputation and Rankings

One critical evaluation of every law school has nothing to do with the current students. It is made by the employers who hire the students and is based on the reputation of the school and its past graduates. This assessment is a product of an employer's experience with graduates of the school, word of mouth, and a look at the rankings put out by different publications and organizations. The most famous of these rankings is put out yearly by *U.S. News and World Report,* but it is not difficult to find similar efforts by companies like Princeton Review or other law school service providers. Your local library or bookstore is likely to have these publications.

These lists are popular sources of information for prospective students, but you should not depend solely on these lists to make judgments about schools. Even the schools that do best in these surveys denounce them as incomplete. As the list makers generally acknowledge, small changes in the weight given to different elements can raise or lower the score of a school significantly. Furthermore, these rankings cannot reflect the subtle variations that lie behind a reputation. These rankings are useful for grouping schools into rough categories, but the difference between number 24 and number 26 is not so great.

One important variation that the rankings miss is the enhanced reputation that a law school may have in a specific region or city. Indeed, only the very top schools enjoy the same respect across the country. You can roughly measure the power of a school's name across the country by looking at where a school's graduates work when they graduate. This information is readily available in the compilations of law school data found in many guidebooks to the country's law schools. Local institutions and their graduates will be known quantities to employers in that area, regardless of the school's standing on the national totem pole. There may be powerful alumni networks in place who will look favorably upon fellow alumni. In addition, schools that are less well known nationally are more likely to focus their education on the law of their state in order to give their students an advantage in the local market (naturally this is a disadvantage if you want to go elsewhere to practice). If you have a good idea of where you want to practice, this local bias can be more valuable than a degree from a nationally known school. On the other hand, if you are unsure where you will live and want to preserve maximum flexibility in your future job prospects, nationally known schools might be better prospects.

A school's enhanced reputation in one market may do little for you if that market slumps when you are seeking a job. While it is difficult to forecast three years in advance, local law job markets are likely to follow the fortunes of the surrounding area. Graduates of law schools in depressed areas may feel the sting, and unfortunately you can't eat prestige. Similarly, the presence of other law schools in the area affects the ability of graduates in the area to find work, no matter how prestigious their school. For example, Boston has six law schools in the immediate vicinity and attracts lawyers from other parts of the country. This reduces the significance of a school's local advantages, because there are so many prospective lawyers in competition with one another. Harry remembers that while interviewing for jobs during the third year, he found it much easier to receive serious attention from out-of-state employers who did not have Boston's luxury of so many home-grown new lawyers appearing each year.

Your Own Rankings

So, how can you get a better idea of your school's reputation than from a list in a magazine? There are a few relatively objective measures that schools (and some of the commercial guides) provide in an attempt to quantify their desirability. You can use these to rank schools according to your own criteria instead of according to what others think is important.

One measure is the number of employers (mainly private firms) that recruit on campus. This number says nothing about the quality of the firms, but it is another rough marker, especially if the school does not attract many on-campus interviewers. This measure is not useful for people interested in non-law-firm jobs, because such employers are unlikely to do much on-campus interviewing anywhere.

Another set of statistics that schools love to emphasize is the average or median starting salary of its graduates and the percentage of graduates employed. Be careful of the latter statistic. It is significant, but pay attention to whether the number is recorded at graduation or at some point, say six months, after graduation. The quality of offers that people accept deteriorates the longer they are out of school, so the first method of measuring provides a better illustration of the success of recent graduates at finding good employment. In addition, the starting salary may be skewed if everyone goes to work in New York (rather than a less expensive city) or if a large percentage of graduates work in public sector or public interest jobs.

Supplementing these statistics with the personal impressions of working lawyers is an excellent idea. Tap any contacts you have in the legal community (such as a firm that often sees graduates from a particular school) and ask for their opinion of the school. Even if they have no idea, they are likely to know someone who does have an informed opinion. Graduates of the school itself may provide some further anecdotal evidence. These efforts are not exactly scientific, but neither is the idea of measuring a school's reputation, so you must expect a high degree of uncertainty.

There are characteristics of law schools other than their reputation that are important to future job hunting. The quality of a school's career counseling and placement office is an extremely practical consideration. Student placement offices can be wonderfully effective and innovative, or they may amount to a pile of ten-year-old biographies of companies stacked in a corner. The more resources a school devotes to its placement office, the more effective it is likely to be. This is an attribute that most books do a particularly poor job of communicating. Every school claims that its placement office is top-notch and staffed by energetic counselors. Check with students at the school to get a more candid assessment of the school's efforts. You could also try to visit the office yourself to check resources and staff, although be aware that its appearance will be dramatically different during the peak recruiting periods in early fall.

If you have strong ideas about the kind of job you want, you can make a more sophisticated analysis of which school will best prepare you for that job. Every school tracks the jobs their graduates take immediately upon graduation, and this information is readily accessible. Does the general flow of people match your expectations? If you want to pursue a public interest career, a school that churns out corporate lawyers should raise warning flags for you. Why does this school specialize in producing a certain kind of lawyers? It may reflect a conscious attempt on the part of the administration, some particularly strong departments within the school, the proclivities of the people who go to that school in the first place, or some combination of all three. Speaking with admissions people may provide some answers to these questions, but interviewing actual students about the campus culture will provide the best insight into the reasons for any channeling into certain areas. More detailed review books may also note these conditions. Keep in mind that people without strong goals regarding their future are the most vulnerable to this shepherding. If your conviction is rock solid, then you have less to fear, but bucking a strong current is never easy.

Academic reputations extend to specific programs as well. A particularly strong individual program may compensate for other deficiencies, but this puts all your eggs in one vulnerable basket. Many programs establish themselves largely through the efforts of one or two professors. If these critical people take a sabbatical at an inopportune time or even leave for another school, they may take the guts of the program with them. Furthermore, you might also discover that Eskimo law is not as enthralling as you had expected or that the market for Eskimo law specialists is not as strong as you had hoped. You are safer focusing on the overall strength of the curriculum.

If the program you desire requires another degree, you should check into the possibility of pursuing a joint degree with the law school and another affiliated institution, such as a business school or a public policy school. Joint degrees are economical and potentially quite valuable, but not every school has such a program in place. Schools will generally publicize any opportunities that students regularly choose, but they may also be amenable to individualized study plans. The admissions office is a good place to ask about any unique ideas you want to try.

Characteristics That Affect Your Quality of Life During Law School

It is largely self-evident that if you attend a law school that tends to match your personality, your chances for academic success increase. The lesson here is that for each school you consider, try to analyze the characteristics of the school, its academic program, its facilities, and its student body, and assess how well they match your own expectations and personality. The better the fit, the better the chances that you will feel comfortable. Reducing the stress that comes with going to law school is an excellent way to ensure that you will make the best effort you can. At the least, you do not want outside, nonschool problems, such as bad living conditions, the lack of a balanced social life, or a teaching style you cannot tolerate, to distract you from your studies.

The years in law school are long enough that quality-of-life factors should be given serious thought. Unfortunately, most quality-of-life factors cannot be quantified in a meaningful way, but there are five factors which stand out:

- school size/class size
- demographics of students and faculty
- facilities
- quality of the faculty
- social life

School Size/Class Size

The size of the school is one of the most important quality-of-life indicators you should consider. Entering classes range from 550 to 600 at the largest schools to around 120 at the smallest schools. The number of your prospective classmates has ramifications on the school's aca-

demic programs and social life that require some thought. The size of a school's class could be a blessing or a curse depending on what you want your law school experience to resemble. Are you accustomed to intimate chats over dinner with your teachers? Do not expect much of that at a large school. Do you have an interest in a particularly esoteric subject? It may well be unavailable at a small school.

The largest schools will not offer the ease in student-faculty contact that is a hallmark of smaller programs. Required classes will contain over a hundred bodies, and professors simply are unable to provide individual attention to most people. This may not bother you, and many people are content to just sit back and listen. Truly motivated students seek out faculty and establish relationships at any size school. Larger schools just require more work to accomplish the same end. The offset to diminished professorial contact *may* come in the form of a larger number of professors and a broader array of available classes (check the faculty size and ratio to students). Smaller schools may well list a wide range of exotic and interesting class titles in their literature; the catch is that many courses may not be offered regularly. Similarly, blocks of material at small schools may rest on the shoulders of one faculty member who may leave, retire, or take a sabbatical.

There is a similar divide in the social consequences of large and small student bodies. Larger classes can be very impersonal, but they are likelier to supply people with whom you genuinely want to study, work, play, and argue (a good thing in the law school context). The number and diversity of extracurricular activities generally has a direct relationship with the number of potential participants. On the other hand, law students are notoriously good at forming new organizations to fill vacuums. If there is an activity you have your heart set on pursuing, you may find others who feel the same way anywhere. Starting from scratch is certainly more work than stepping into an established group, but these are activities that spawn great resumes. Look at your own university background and subsequent social patterns. What sounds like the better fit?

Demographics of Students and Faculty

The demographics of the class provide invaluable insight into the learning environment and social experience of a school. The average age of the entering class, which is often overlooked, will have important social consequences (older groups are more likely to have significant interests outside of law school). While the numbers of minorities and women attending law school have continued to rise, there are still significant variations in representation of minorities and women among schools. The presence of a diverse student body may be a critical element of your support network and provide a significant social and extracurricular outlet. Faculty demographics speak to the same issue. The number of faculty members who are women or members of minority groups is one indication of the administration's commitment to providing a diverse experience, although the raw number of nonwhite, nonmale professors is likely to be low at any law school. Minority or female faculty members may be invaluable mentors for many students, and these professors are also more likely to focus on race or gender issues in class. Still, this is a crude means of judging how the school will serve your needs. If possible, look beyond the bare statistics on representation and confer with people at the school. The admissions office should be able to give you contacts with people or organizations that you can use to get a more detailed picture of the environment.

Facilities

Facilities are another factor that appears to be quantifiable, but in reality the numbers can be extremely difficult to interpret without additional investigation. Library size is an excellent example of this problem. The raw number of volumes may impress you, but for many students libraries in law schools are more useful as quiet and comfortable study environments than as containers of books. If you generally never use the library, it may make no difference whatsoever to your law school experience. An actual look at the library will speak volumes. Can you see yourself working there? Is it open when you are likely to use it? The rise of on-line and computer research devices has made the size of a law library less important, particularly if the school does not require a long research project.

Indeed, the presence and availability of computer resources and on-line databases are more important to legal education and the future skills of lawyers than the existence of thousands of books. Many of today's law students have become so enamored of computer research that they devote little attention to the books that were so vital in the past. Ideally, students should have access to on-line research tools from their own rooms, not just on one or two terminals at the library. Visiting the campus facilities or talking with the students is very helpful for understanding the true state of affairs in this critical area.

Other facilities may in practice be far more important to you than the library. Convenience, economy, and, perhaps most important, sociability make housing a significant consideration. The need for the law school to provide housing varies widely depending on the surrounding locale. The quality and availability of law student housing runs from nonexistent to plush locations on campus. Again, word of mouth will be a better source than the descriptions in the law school pamphlets as to the true state of affairs. Are the lecture halls comfortable? Is there a pleasant place where students can hang out? Is there access to a gym or any other entertainment facilities? None of these considerations are likely to be deal-breakers, but the cumulative effect of the physical plant is worthy of note.

Quality of the Faculty

The strength of the faculty is also important, but reports on the general teaching ability of a faculty are hard to find. Some law schools compile student reactions to professors as an aid to their students choosing classes. These may provide some insight as to general student attitudes toward their professors. A few schools make teaching ability an explicit criterion in hiring and tenure decisions, but generally teaching prowess is secondary to publishing credentials. The vague generalities that appear in guidebooks will rarely provide much assistance in obtaining a sense of the general teaching aptitude.

The presence of big names among the faculty does not guarantee that you will interact meaningfully with them. Star professors may not be available to students outside of class hours because of the crush of people seeking their time or by their own choice (high-priced consulting may seem more rewarding to them than the gratis counseling of first-year students). They also may leave for greener pastures. Finally, every school has its good professors, so unless you are dying to work with a specific god of civil procedure, individual teachers are unlikely to make one school appreciably better than another. Furthermore, as both Harry and Chris discovered, the most famous professors are not necessarily the best teachers; they may simply have published the most articles.

It is also difficult to distinguish overall academic programs because of the pervasiveness of the case method and the similarity of academic schedules and requirements. For example, the first-year curriculum is virtually identical across the country. The biggest difference in academics lies in the national schools' preference for general theory and other schools' focus on one state's laws. A few programs do offer significantly different learning approaches, such as a strong internship program or an extra emphasis on legal research and writing. Schools with these different approaches display them prominently in their propaganda. The trick is to do enough research so that you come across the array of possibilities.

Social Life

A final set of factors might loosely be labeled campus culture. Does the student body enjoy a social life? Is there an enormous sense of pressure or competition between students? Is there a strong ideological leaning? If you had solid answers to these questions, they would be quite useful. Who would want to go to a school where the prevailing norm demanded total abstinence from a social life or supported general backstabbing of your classmates? The often subjective nature of these inquiries makes it hard to discover clear-cut answers. Competition between students is impossible to quantify. At best, you get an individual's opinion or a synthesis of some opinions (which are not necessarily representative opinions) from a guidebook.

There are a few marginally more objective ways of testing what books or others might tell you. Take a look at the surrounding locale. If the school is located in the middle of an interesting area, it may make little difference to you if the school serves as a center of social activity. Does the school have a campus community or a student gathering place? If students have to commute, it is less likely they will stay to socialize. The presence of, or perhaps the lack of, student organizations espousing various ideological stands is one indicator of the ideological tilt of a law school.

Ultimately, the importance of the campus culture for you depends upon your own personality. Larger schools provide more opportunities to find people searching for the same mix of social life and academic intensity that you would like, but every school will have people generally sympathetic to your approach to law school. These qualities make for better gossip material about rival schools than they do as vital considerations in your choice of law schools.

GATHERING INFORMATION ON LAW SCHOOLS

You are probably familiar with the basic ways of gathering information from your college search days, but conduct your law school investigation with more vigor. The stakes and potential benefits are high, and it behooves you to use all the resources at your disposal before making such a significant investment.

The first steps for most people are to peruse national rankings from different sources, talk with friends facing the same ritual, and skim a few of the general resources on law schools for ideas. Many people never go beyond this, reasoning that they will do more research if they are accepted by more than one place. This approach both wastes money and runs the serious risk that you might miss a school that would be good for you but that is not covered by list makers.

Interview Students, Past or Present

You should supplement your initial scan of the law school market by interviewing past and present students from different law schools. Everyone loves to pass down wisdom to people "intelligent enough" to ask their opinions. The primary difficulty lies in motivating yourself to actually seek out these people.

Where do you find them? You can run down your list of friends, relatives, friends of relatives, relatives of friends, and so on. This is convenient but hardly systematic. Try your college guidance counselor or pre-law adviser early in the admissions process. While the quality of pre-law advisers varies greatly, a good one can be an invaluable ally in the application process. Even with less helpful advisers, the sooner you realize the state of affairs the better. Good counselors can provide valuable references and impart the accumulated wisdom of watching many others in your shoes. In particular, they may know recent graduates who are currently at your target schools. Think about what is important to you ahead of time so you can ask specific questions.

Talk to the Admissions Staff

Admissions staff from individual schools are also good resources, although the degree of candor and usefulness depends highly on the individual representative. There simply are not enough personnel at most law schools to provide individual interviews for either information or admission, but the schools try to redress this by sending their people out on the road. Many college career offices organize visits by representatives of law schools to give talks and answer questions. Law school fairs held in major cities attract large numbers of prospective students and representatives from a wide range of schools. These opportunities, particularly the fairs, are extremely economical means of getting detailed information on a wide range of schools. After all, if you can bring the mountain to you, why should you pay to go visit the mountain?

Visit the Campus

Visiting every potential school requires more effort and expense than it is worth at this stage of the application process. Law school campuses tend to be small, often just one building. While it is nice to see the facilities and the surrounding city, it may make more economic sense to wait until you are accepted before you visit. Telephone conversations with a few students can give you the critical information on what most people think of the safety of the surrounding area, the usefulness of the library and computing facilities, and anything else you would see on a tour. Admissions offices will often maintain lists of students or alumni available to speak to prospective applicants. On the other hand, if the campus is convenient, then check it out. Contact the admissions office, and see what organized tours they have and if they give informational interviews. If nothing else, wandering around campus is a good way to casually meet and observe the student body.

You are the only person who can decide the priority of the factors in your wish list of schools. Once you have decided what is important to you, make your research systematic and thorough. The effort will not be wasted. While cost and admissions prospects will probably prune your list, separating the considerations will give you a clearer sense of the trade-offs you may have to make and help you to choose the lucky schools that will receive your application.

11

WHICH LAW SCHOOLS MIGHT ACCEPT YOU?

Once you have figured out which law schools best meet your academic and social desires, you will have to swallow hard and calculate whether *you* meet the academic and social criteria of the law schools you like. In other words, where can you get in?

This question causes as much angst as anything else in the law school application process. Unbounded optimism mixes with cold despair and centers most people around a happy (or unhappy) medium. The truth is that there are pretty good ways to estimate your likely range of schools, but there are too many people with roughly equal credentials applying at any given level of school to get any more specific than that. The intangibles easily outweigh the known quantities, and no generic explanation of law school admission procedures can help. There is, however, great value in locating the likely range of schools that may accept you. It helps you to focus your efforts and makes your application process more efficient and economical. You should still investigate and apply to some schools at which you consider yourself a long shot. You just want to make sure that not every school you try is a long shot.

As we pointed out in Chapter 10, you need to figure out which schools are best suited for you before you pare the list down on competitive and financial grounds. Considering a wide range of institutions ensures that you have thought about what is important to you and ensures you have not missed a diamond in the rough. Now you can move on to examining the schools that interest you with a more critical eye towards practicality. This chapter examines how you analyze your chances of being accepted at your chosen schools. Chapter 12 looks at

116

the financial realities of attending law school. These additional screening processes will whittle your wish list to a manageable number (Chapter 14 discusses how many schools constitute a manageable number).

HOW LAW SCHOOLS
PROCESS APPLICATIONS

Every law school receives hundreds, if not thousands, of applications and supporting material every fall. The most exclusive schools have more than ten applicants for each slot, and even less competitive schools will have hundreds more applicants than they can take. This presents a fundamental problem. Law schools have too many applications and too few staff members to make as thorough an assessment of each individual as they would like.

The application review process reflects the best efforts of the law schools to cope with this sea of paper. Each school follows its own procedures. These systems differ in three major ways:

*   when the application file is reviewed
*   how the application file is screened
*   who reviews the application file

The first difference is the major distinction. Some schools practice a rolling admissions policy: files are reviewed shortly after they are received, and offers for class slots are made as soon as possible. At the other extreme, some schools wait until the final application date before they read files and extend offers. This difference is important because there is a significant advantage to applying earlier in the application cycle at schools that use rolling admissions. Chapter 14 discusses this advantage further.

The other two major differences in application review processes are much less important from the applicant's perspective because they make no difference in how or when you complete the application. Most schools employ some kind of screening system to save time: support staff will weed out some of the weakest applications or ensure that tough calls receive more scrutiny. Some schools even allow the screening personnel to automatically admit candidates who have scores above set benchmarks. The actual admissions committee may consist of a single dean personally reading every application or an elaborate combination of professors and admissions officers collaborating in committees. Some schools even let law students assist in the process.

You can find out more detail about an individual law school's approach if you wish. The application materials and some of the guides to law schools provide some descriptions of each school's process. In particular, the timing of a school's offers of acceptance (rolling admissions or other practice) is contained in the application materials. Candid answers about who reads the files once they enter the law school gates are more likely to come from individual members of the admissions staff than in the published material. Questions at law school fairs or during visits to the admissions office are the best means of getting specifics. The usefulness of this information is questionable, however. Quite frankly, the exact sequence any school follows is not that important to you. Individual quirks are unlikely to be so pronounced that you could tailor your application to somehow take advantage of a particular admissions officer or screening process.

APPLICATION ELEMENTS THAT LAW SCHOOLS EMPHASIZE

The wall of paper confronting admissions personnel inspires a certain amount of despair among admissions officers. They need some means of sifting out the worthy from the pretenders while retaining their eyesight and sanity. The quick and dirty method that law schools use to screen candidates is by looking at the applicant's LSAT scores and GPA. Candidates whose scores in these categories are at or above the school's average are sure to have their applications read carefully. Candidates whose scores are below that average will have to prove to the admissions committee that there is a compelling reason to ignore these important benchmarks.

Obviously, there are elements to the law school application other than the LSAT and GPA, but these two bits of information will pigeonhole almost everyone into a certain caliber of law school. Chapter 14 explains all the elements of the application more thoroughly and discusses their relative importance for you. Understanding how law schools depend upon the LSAT score and undergraduate GPA, however, will go a long way to helping you understand how competitive your application is going to be at a given school.

How LSAT Scores and Grades Are Evaluated—The Index Number

Many law schools have simplified their screening process by creating a formula that condenses an applicant's LSAT score, cumulative undergraduate GPA, and possibly other modifiers into one number. Every application receives an index score based on these components. The scoring of the LSAT (from 120 to 180) is designed to make this conversion more convenient (dropping the 100 gives a score between 20 and 80, which can then be divided by 20 to give a score between 1 and 4, paralleling the grading systems of most schools). Each school tries hard to ensure that its index formula accurately measures who will excel at the school. This strategy allows administrative assistants to do the grunt work of routing the applications on the basis of easily quantifiable scores and allows the admissions officers to pay more attention to applications that are not easy yes or no candidates. The gains in efficiency ease the pain of losing a few people in the cracks of the system.

The Law School Data Assembly Service (LSDAS) actually computes the index number for many law schools according to a formula that each school decides upon individually. The LSDAS serves as a clearinghouse for almost every law school. Schools that use the LSDAS require that all their applicants subscribe to the service. Prospective students send in some basic biographical information and a transcript to LSDAS (generally at the same time they register for the LSAT), which then sends a summary of the information and the student's LSAT results and transcript to the law schools. One wrinkle is that the LSDAS has its own system for calculating GPA, which may be different from the method that your college uses. This can result in a small discrepancy between what you think your GPA is and what the law schools think it is, but it should not be a significant difference.

Problems with the Index

The indexing system is not perfect by any stretch of the imagination. Remember, this is an efficiency device; it is not designed to discover the diamonds in the rough. One major limitation of unmodified indexing is that it treats all undergraduate grades as being equal, while it is clear that they are not. A 4.0 GPA at Podunk State does not mean the same thing as a 4.0 GPA at an ivy-laden institution. Many schools try to account for this problem by modifying the index number to reflect the quality of the undergraduate school. This may be done formally, by giving it a numerical weight that is factored into the equation, or informally, where officers may give an edge to graduates of some schools with better reputations. This is only a partial solution, as the weight given to different schools is inexact, particularly if the law school does not see many applicants from a particular school or if a college is improving rapidly.

There is an additional problem with the index. After all, a 4.0 GPA in a challenging curriculum at Podunk State could actually mean more than a 4.0 at the ivy-laden institution earned through a variety of classes taught by professors who never saw a grade they didn't want to inflate. This problem is a difficult one, since admissions officers are unlikely to understand all the nuances and grading policies of the courses at any given school. The LSDAS helps a bit by ranking the grade-point average of everyone from the same school who subscribes to the service that year. This form of class rank lets admissions officers know if *everyone* at some school has an A– average, so people from schools with rampant grade inflation do not have an inordinate advantage. Unfortunately, neither the virtuous who take a rigorous course load nor the slackers who take the easy road are likely to receive their just deserts in the law school application. The virtuous will have to take comfort in their moral purity and the benefits of a more stringent course load that we discussed in Chapter 8.

The root of the problem with the index is that the idea of trying to wrap up the whole application in one number is absurd. Law schools are aware of this limitation and do their best to ensure that the formula reflects the actual success rate of graduates from any college as closely as possible. After all, they do not want to lose good candidates for admission any more than you want to be lost.

The good news is that no law school relies entirely upon their index. The index number channels applications; it does not reject them. While an application may be read by fewer people if it has a low index score, it will be read. People who do poorly on raw scores may compensate in other ways. Conversely, a high index score does not always guarantee admission.

HOW TO ASSESS YOUR
ATTRACTIVENESS TO LAW SCHOOLS

What works for the law schools as rough indicators of your probability of acceptance will also work for you. You will not know the exact formula any law school uses, but you do not need to. There are enough data in promotional materials and guidebooks to provide a decent picture of your admission odds (not certainties, but odds) at any school, *if you know what your own scores are.* Making these calculations before you get your LSAT scores back considerably complicates the picture (which is one good reason to take the test early). You can approximate your score based on your practice exam results, but this only gives you a rough idea. You might be significantly higher or lower, so you will have to consider a wider range of schools then you might otherwise.

LSAT Score/GPA Profile Grids

LSAT score/GPA admissions profile tables are the best widely available resource to help you determine your odds. Some, but not all, schools compile and make available grids that track the success rates of applicants with different combinations of LSAT scores and GPAs. The grids have ranges of LSAT scores (e.g., 160–165) on one axis and ranges of GPAs (e.g., 3.25–3.49) on the other. The grid contains the number of applications and acceptances for each combination of scores and grades. *The Official Guide to U.S. Law Schools,* which is published by the Law School Admission Council, compiles as many of these tables as are available. In addition, many schools include their grid in their promotional materials. These charts give much more information than the median LSAT scores and GPAs of entering classes, which are also widely available. Study these tables if they are available for your target schools.

There are several messages that emerge from these grids. First, the LSAT scores and GPAs are excellent indicators of success at the application game. This should be no surprise, but look closer. There may be a score below which the school simply does not take anyone. The school may place more emphasis on one score than another. You can also get a rough idea of the competition you will face by looking at the numbers of applicants at different combinations of scores.

The second major lesson of these charts is that your GPA and LSAT score are not everything. Every school has a number of people who are above the school's average in both departments who are not accepted. This reflects the subjectivity so prevalent in the application game and the overall competition for law school slots. You will have a strong temptation to look at your own background and accomplishments and adjust your odds of success accordingly. This is not a bad idea, as long as you recognize that there are limits to how much your other qualities will transcend low scores and that some factors are easier to quantify than others when you assess your chances.

Adjusting Your Place on the LSAT/Grades Grid

There are many possible explanations why an individual with below-average LSAT scores or grades might get into a certain law school while another person with above-average scores might be rejected. There are four broad categories of factors that might explain this phenomenon:

- reputation of undergraduate institution
- demographics (e.g., race, gender, age, socioeconomic background)
- extracurricular activities or post-collegiate experience
- quality of application

The LSAT/grades grids do not show how any of these factors influence an admissions officer's decision, but these are the kind of factors that will make a law school look beyond a candidate's poor scores. These factors can work against an applicant as well, so the person with great scores but no extracurricular activities who writes a poor application is likely to feel rejection's sting. Unfortunately, it is generally very difficult to quantify the effect of any of these factors with any kind of precision. You can only make some rough guesses as to how much any of these nonquantifiable adjustments will help or hurt you.

Reputation of Undergraduate Institution

One major limitation of the tables is that they do not reveal the undergraduate institutions of the applicants. Not surprisingly, this is an important consideration. A 3.5 GPA at a community college is not the same as a 3.5 at one of the best schools in the country. Law schools take this fact into account, so this is one explanation for the lack of success of some candidates with higher-than-average GPAs.

You probably have a general impression of the strength of your undergraduate institution's name, but you may be able to get more specific information. Some colleges track the acceptance rate of their undergrads at different law schools. Check with your college career counseling office to see if they keep these kinds of records and make them available. If you are lucky, the college may even have information about its members' LSAT scores, GPAs, age, gender, minority status, or other factors. This is a great way to understand the discrepancies in the admissions tables.

You can glean a little information about how well your college's graduates do at a given law school even if your college does not keep good track of its undergrads' success rates. Many law schools compile lists of the colleges that are represented in their ranks. While the numbers from each school may not be available, the absence of your school from such a list is probably not a good sign. Talk with anyone who might have inside information. Your pre-law tutor may have seen enough applications or talked to enough admissions officers from different schools to have some ideas. If this approach fails, question any admissions people you can. They will never discourage anyone from applying to their law school, but they may be able to give you some candid answers about your chances.

Demographics

The effect of your background and demographics on your chances for admission is undeniably important. As a general rule, today's law schools try hard to accept a diverse class of students from all walks of society, who bring different life experiences to the school. While it is difficult to quantify what effect being a member of a minority group might have upon your admissions chances, it is likely to help your odds. In addition, if there are fewer candidates from a certain demographic group applying to a school, members of that group may have a relative advantage compared to the rest of the pool as the law school strives to preserve the diversity of the class.

Some of this search for diversity is institutionalized in specific admissions policies. For example, public law schools prefer to accept their own state residents over people from other states. Law schools also may have special admissions programs for candidates from racial minority groups who might not make the cut otherwise. Each school's program is different and may change from year to year, so you should inquire at the admissions office if you might qualify for such a program. There are not usually special admissions programs for people who belong to other minority groups, such as gender, religion, socioeconomic status, sexual orientation, country of origin, or any other possible dividing category, but this does not mean that law school admissions officers are not searching hard for promising candidates from these minority groups. Given the relatively diverse group of law school applicants today, it is unlikely that identifying yourself in any one of these minority groups will by itself adjust your odds of success.

Extracurricular Activities and Job Experience

You might be tempted to make a small upward adjustment in your expectation level if you have great work or extracurricular experience, but this is not a dependable upward adjustment unless you are searching for extra shelf space to put your Nobel prize next to your Heisman. It is likely that people applying to the same quality of school with comparable scores and academic backgrounds will also have done something else with their lives, and their resumes will reflect it. This is not to say that your nonacademic experiences will not help you; they will. But they are more likely to improve your chances within the range of schools that your scores place you in than to make you a good candidate at a school that normally would not accept those scores.

You should also not worry about rumors that one person's influence or contacts with an authority figure at the law school helped them beat the odds. Admissions officers are probably not totally blind to $100,000 "donations," but the proportion of people willing and able to make them is quite small. Mere friendship with a dean or another admissions officer should not be the basis of your application either; it is a distinct long shot. In a word, use whatever connections you have, but do not depend on them.

Quality of Application

Finally, do not hope that your application will be so good as to stun admissions officers into ignoring your credentials. The application is important, but by itself it simply is not going to carry the day. Make your calculations based on the assumption that you will do a thorough, conscientious job on the application, which will give you as good a chance as you deserve. You should also assume that virtually everyone else will also do everything right. Law students as a group are overachieving, well organized, and slightly anal people. They will not make your life easier by applying late en masse. This adds a bit of pressure (get used to it) to perform your best in this process and not screw up.

So, now you have looked at your own qualifications and background, judged them against the standards evidenced at the schools that most interested you based solely on their merits, and weeded out the ones that appear out of reach. What next? The last hurdle, just as in the rest of life, is money.

12

WHICH LAW SCHOOLS CAN YOU AFFORD?

An ugly, ugly prospect for many people who are already burdened with undergraduate loans is the prospect of a new round of tuition payments. Even people without outstanding debt from college gag at the prospect of paying $100,000 over three years (at the most expensive schools) for the honor of working incredibly hard. If this number does not make you think seriously about why you are going to law school, nothing will. Unless you are fortunate enough to have saved money or get financial help, you will have significant debt upon graduation. Your future employment plans and style of living will bow before this albatross. Are you prepared to write out a check for $10,000 for your first semester?

Fortunately there are ways to reduce the hit on your wallet. There are less expensive schools and programs within schools that cost less. You can get financial aid, grants, and scholarships. You can also earn some income while you are in law school. Taking advantage of these strategies entails sacrificing some combination of time, opportunity, or prestige but can make a critical difference in the amount you have to invest in your legal career.

Accordingly, after you have decided which schools you would like to attend and which could actually accept you, you must decide which schools you can afford to attend. It may simply be too expensive to go to the school you would like, even if you have a great shot at getting in the door. You will have to inspect the schools remaining on your list (and perhaps rethink a few you had discarded) to make sure that they work for you financially. This may require some additional digging,

126

since not all the information you may need will be easily accessible, and not every school offers every money-saving technique.

Your law degree is a long-term asset, and you should think of your investment in it in the same way. Remember to consider your enhanced earnings capacity upon graduation. This is another time to check the employment and average salary statistics of your candidate schools, bearing in mind that these are rough indicators and that they depend heavily upon what kind of job you take upon graduation. If you want to pursue a legal career that pays less straight out of school, you will have to budget accordingly.

HOW MUCH LAW SCHOOL COSTS

You can figure out the price tag of any school relatively easily. Tuition figures are provided in the standard guides to law schools and by the schools themselves. Naturally, you will have to account for your living expenses, but many law schools provide average figures for the typical additional costs, such as room, board, books, and transportation. Even if an individual institution does not provide the information, you can generalize from other schools that do provide it, especially if they are located in the same city. Keep a budget of your current expenses to get an idea of what kind of lifestyle you can expect to lead and how much or little you might be able to shave. The end total will give you a yearly figure for each school.

Public Law Schools

Your estimate will be a startlingly high figure for most institutions, but not all. Public law schools can be great deals. Some of the "public ivies" are as well respected as any private school at a fraction of the price. Even state schools that do not draw nationally are likely to have excellent reputations within the state. However, you will have to qualify as a state resident to take advantage of the lower tuition rates. After all, you lose one-third of the benefit of your bargain if it takes a year to meet the residency requirements. Check all the state rules and loopholes on eligibility; you may be able to qualify immediately with some foresight and luck.

Unfortunately, public schools are not the solution for everyone. Many of the best institutions are proudly private and charge accordingly. The competition for slots at public law schools is intense precisely because they are such a bargain.

Another way to spend less on law school is to enter a degree program that takes fewer than three years. Unfortunately, there are only a few such options available to a limited number of people. A few law schools will accept students from an affiliated undergraduate institution after their third year of college. This cuts off one year of academic payments, although not exactly from law school. Joint degree programs are more popular and easier to plan, but many people want only a law degree.

Part-Time Law School Programs

Part-time programs present an attractive option for reducing the burden of law school costs. Around sixty law schools have such programs, which allow students to devote more time to earning money during their law school years than traditional full-time programs do. These part-time programs fill an important niche by allowing people to attend law school who otherwise might not be able to afford it or who might not have the time to devote themselves to a full-time course of study. The latter advantage is particularly important for those who are considering law as a second career or who have family or other commitments that do not allow them to dedicate themselves totally to the pursuit of a law degree.

Part-time students cover the same material and have the same academic requirements to graduate as do their full-time counterparts. The primary difference is that the classes are held at night, on weekends, and during the summer so that students can hold down a full-time job or otherwise meet other time commitments. This structure spreads the course work over a longer time period (at least four years) so that the students can manage their time demands better.

Part-time programs allow their students to borrow less money or even pay for school as they go. In addition, if the student hopes to combine law with another field (a common desire), the student may advance a career in the other field while simultaneously developing legal skills. Part-time students receive the same caliber of instruction and classes as do full-time students at the same law school, since the classes are the same and the professors are drawn from the same faculty that teaches the full-time classes. Part-time students tend to be older than those enrolled full-time, which presents an interesting array of life experience to all and an extra comfort level for older students.

Part-time programs, however, should not be taken lightly by those who have enough time and money to attend law school full-time. There are some disadvantages to part-time programs. Studying law while working full-time is a grueling process, where you work a full day, go to class for a few hours in the evening, and then need a few more hours to do your reading for the next day. Weekends are spent playing catch-up. Everyone is in the same position, so at least you are not penalized for the time demands as you would be if you tried to pursue the same outside commitment in a full-time program, but there are other hidden costs. There is the opportunity cost of the extra year spent studying rather than working at a lawyer's salary, the threat that you may lack the energy or time to fully benefit from the teaching, and the effect on your quality of life. Extracurricular activities suffer as well. There is not enough time to take advantage of all the organizations and other non-classroom experiences that law school has to offer. Finally, you do not get the advantage of summers off to try work experience in different legal settings, so there is less opportunity to explore different career paths during law school. In sum, the negatives of trying to work full-time while studying law part-time are numerous enough that unless it is truly a necessity you should try to avoid putting yourself in that position.

HOW TO HELP COVER THE COST OF LAW SCHOOL

When analyzing the cost of the various law schools you are considering, you may well wonder, "How am I going to pay for *any* of these schools?" Most law students foot their bills at least partly with the financial support of family. Beyond that, many students tap into savings earned from pre-law work experiences. Even taking into account those two sources of funds, you may still face an appreciable gap between your financial resources and the cost of your target law schools. The most common ways to bridge this gap are money earned *during* law school and financial aid from institutions.

Working During Law School

It is hardly a revelation that the more money you can earn during your three years of school, the less you will have to pay back. You will want to get an idea of what you may earn during school to help you decide which law school you can afford. The answer depends on what jobs you can get and what jobs you want to get, but it is quite possible to earn as much as $25,000 in a year and attend school at the same time. Most people will not earn nearly this much, but there are combinations of jobs that allow many to put themselves through law school without accumulating staggering loans.

Summer Jobs

The extremely lucrative summer employment opportunities available to law students account for most of the money that people earn during their law school days. Since most law schools do not even offer summer classes, students are generally free to work as summer clerks or associates in law-related jobs (which we discussed in Chapter 5).

Students who work summers at private firms can be paid extravagant amounts of money. Summer associates in the best firms in large cities earn easily over $1,000 per week. For example, the current summer rate at the best firms in New York City is $1,500 per week. Over a twelve- or fourteen-week summer this can translate into some major savings if you practice any self-restraint on expenditures.

However, think about your odds of getting one of these high-paying jobs before you depend on that type of income. Not surprisingly, the competition for the high-paying summer jobs is intense. The ability of a school's students to get high-paying summer jobs is closely correlated with the prestige of the institution. An informal survey of some students currently at the school about the kinds of jobs people take during the summers will give a better picture of your likely financial opportunities.

You should also be aware that law firms strongly prefer hiring second-year students, which results in a dearth of high-paying opportunities for people during the first summer and leaves only one summer during law school where you have a reasonable chance to earn some respectable money. The reasons for the preference for second-year students are clear. First, law firms are better able to judge your legal aptitude when they can look at your first-year grades and your previous work experience (and that cannot be done in the midst of the first year, before the new law students have any significant grades to report). The top firms only want to give offers to the best and brightest, so they need to know how you rank in your law school class. Second, it is more likely that the best and brightest will want to return full-time after graduation to the firms where they worked after their second year, so firms are reluctant to pay much attention to those who will not graduate for another two years.

This all means that you should be extremely wary about planning on getting on the summer associate gravy train after your first year of law school. Chris witnessed many of his classmates scrambling desperately for one of the few slots at the high-paying firms available to first-year students.

Things get even tougher financially in the summer if you are not interested in pursuing a position in a large private firm. Sadly enough, most other lines of work do not pay anywhere near the salaries that summer associates at the blue-chip law firms command. Other common summer jobs, such as working for professors or in public interest organizations, pay subsistence wages, if that. Harry spent the summer after his first year working for a solo practitioner, who graciously allowed Harry to perform the most menial legal tasks for absolutely no salary whatsoever. The experience was helpful, but it did not help with the immediate bills. Harry remembers some other classmates who had to take nonlaw summer jobs, such as working as a department store clerk, because they could not find a summer position that used their new legal skills. At least *they* earned cold cash that could replenish their barren bank accounts.

Working During the School Year

There are, of course, nine other months of the year to make money. Many students have worked during college and hope to do it again in law school. This is possible, but as we mentioned in connection with part-time law school programs, the difficulty of finding enough time to study properly while working enough hours to put a significant dent in your tuition payments goes up exponentially in law school. The difference between law school and college is the sheer number of hours that law students feel the need to devote to studying. Most people feel compelled to spend much more time reading, reviewing, and outlining than they did as undergraduates. In particular, test periods become all-consuming. Your law school performance is too important to your future career prospects to approach it any other way. If you try to burn the candle at both ends, your grades will suffer. Furthermore, you are seriously handicapping yourself in relation to your peers if you are trying to work twenty hours a week more than they are. This is another good subject to probe with current students or admissions personnel. They will have a good idea of how common it is, and how lucrative it is, for people to hold down jobs during law school.

Concerns about time management have prompted many law schools to discourage students from holding down any job while school is in session, particularly first-year students. Also, anything that adds stress to your life will not be welcome, particularly in your first year, when the unknowns and the pressure are at their peak. Working a substantial number of hours also forecloses the opportunity to get involved in extracurricular activities or to otherwise enjoy the law school experience.

This gloomy picture should not completely discourage you from working during law school; you just cannot assume that you will earn more than a few thousand dollars a semester. As your ability to handle your academic workload efficiently increases over time, more opportunities present themselves. Academic campuses provide some jobs that accommodate the study patterns and extracurricular demands of law students. Some of these, such as student teaching positions or working as assistants for professors, can also provide different insights into law. Harry, for example, earned some spending money during his second year by serving as a counselor to students in the first-year writing program. If a law school is linked to an undergraduate college, there may be teaching or counseling jobs at the college for which law students are well suited. Some law firms will hire law students, particularly those who have worked as summer associates with the firm, to do part-time work over the school year. Just as with summer jobs, it is easier to get these jobs after your first year of law school. Teaching and counseling jobs will often be filled the prior year. Professors prefer to hire students with more legal experience. All these types of work help bring in needed cash and provide useful learning opportunities. Still, the amount that you are likely to make from these jobs will not make much of a dent in your overall law school bills.

Financial Aid

The bulk of financial assistance to law students comes in the form of loans, of which there are three main sources:

- the federal government
- institutional loans from the school itself
- loans from private sources

You should become familiar with the characteristics of all three sources to take best advantage of what is out there before you submit your applications. The lines between the three sources are often blurred, because law school financial aid offices are instrumental in distributing federal loan money and may even help arrange private loans for those who need them.

Government Loans

At present, federal government financial assistance for law students comes in two main forms: Perkins loans and Stafford loans. The generous terms of the loans and the possibility of government payments of interest dictate that you should look to these loans first.

The Perkins loan is a need-based loan for which the government pays the interest while you are enrolled at least half-time. The law schools distribute the money for the government. The amount of money available under the Perkins depends on the institution you attend, but the most you can receive is $5,000 per year.

There are two types of Stafford loans: a need-based version under which the government pays interest, and a non-need-based loan for which the student is responsible for the interest. You may borrow up to $18,500 per year under the Stafford program.

To be eligible for either loan you must satisfy a citizenship requirement, not have defaulted on other federal loans, attend school at least half-time, make satisfactory academic progress towards a degree, and meet your Selective Service requirements.

In order to qualify for either a Perkins or a Stafford loan, you must complete the Free Application for Federal Student Aid (FAFSA). You can get the FAFSA either at a college career center or by calling the Department of Education (1-800-433-3243). Some law schools will send it to you when you apply. If you have technical questions about the form, call the Department of Education.

Approximately four to six weeks after you file the FAFSA, the Department of Education will evaluate your application and send you a Student Aid Report (SAR). The SAR is required by the law schools so they can determine exactly what federal aid you can receive and so they can tailor the rest of your financial aid package. Therefore, although the deadline for FAFSA applications is in early May, you want to complete it much sooner so that it does not delay your entire financial aid determination procedure. The best time to acquire a copy of the FAFSA is in December or January.

Institutional Loans

The law schools use the FAFSA and your answers to their own financial assistance forms to determine your eligibility for a combination of federal and institutional loans. The terms of these institutional loans are also more generous than those on the private market. The schools can also be more flexible than the federal government. If your individual circumstances do not fall neatly into the requirements of the government loan programs, the school will still be able to adapt to your unique needs. The forms and requirements for institutional loans differ by school.

The major problem with institutional loans is that their availability depends entirely on the depth of the school's pockets, which varies greatly. The availability of the money for the individual applicant will also vary depending on when the application is considered. Just as a school's admission criteria can get higher as the number of slots decline during the acceptance process, the flexibility and generosity of the financial aid office will decline the later you enter the game. There simply may not be any money left to lend if you are the last in line. An early application is the best defense against this unfortunate possibility.

So, how do law schools determine who gets the money? There are several considerations financial aid officers make for each candidate, but law schools determine your financial need via a basic formula that subtracts your resources from the school's estimate of a yearly budget. The school then uses its determination of your financial need as the basis for your assistance package.

Note that the school, not you, will determine how much money it will take to study, live, and eat in a given year at their law school. These numbers are usually published in the school's promotional material. The schools will be fair, but their budgets are on the lean side. Those who are accustomed, or who want to be accustomed, to a more luxurious lifestyle will have to make up the difference themselves, because schools will not extend extra aid without a compelling reason, such as surgery or children. A related limitation on a law school's generosity is that it cannot consider your current consumer debt because of federal requirements that the loan money be related to your education, not for paying off the debt on your stereo. Some schools will allow loans to be used for major law school purchases, such as computer equipment, but you should check with the financial aid office before you assume that extraordinary expenses are covered.

If you have extenuating circumstances that make it clear that you need particular attention in drawing up your budget, you must let the law school's financial aid office know. It is common for law students to have dependents, such as spouses, children, or other family members, and law schools are used to dealing with the particular constraints this puts on your budget. Other extraordinary factors that make a difference in the amount of aid you need, such as a family illness or extended unemployment, should be documented as far as possible and communicated to the school.

There are also a few wrinkles in the way different institutions determine your level of resources. You may expect that estimating your resources is as easy as counting to zero (or even less if you are carrying debt from college), but you may have more assets than you think. In particular, law schools and other sources of financial aid generally expect some parental contribution to your tuition (one important exception to this rule is that the federal loans will treat you as being independent from your parents). The expected contribution will vary according to your family's size, number of children in college, savings, and income. The schools will require your parents' tax information to make these determinations, so you may need to convince your parents to file their returns early so you can apply for financial aid early. While this does not foreclose the possibility that your parents will not contribute money toward your legal education, financial aid officers will act as if you had the contribution for the purposes of determining how much aid you will receive. Law schools allow students to prove their independence from their family, but these requirements are often quite stringent and very difficult for someone straight out of college to meet.

There are other variables in the resource equation, such as how much, if any, money the law school will assume you will make during your summer vacations or how your aid changes from one year to the next. The key is to read the fine print of the loan materials the law school sends out and to ask as many questions as possible so you can avoid pitfalls or take advantage of any opportunities that present themselves. You are the only one who cares enough about the result to think through all the possibilities.

Private Loans

The final major source of financial aid is private banks and lenders. These private institutions will provide better rates for student loans than you would get as a mere consumer. Private lenders are the source of last resort for many people who do not qualify for need-based loans or who cannot get enough assistance otherwise, because the loan terms, not surprisingly, are the least favorable. Private sources may require some combination of a higher interest rate, a guaranty, a co-signer, or origination fees. They are not need-based. On the other hand, these loans are generally available to those with a decent credit history and do not operate on the same tight time schedule as the schools do, although there may be a point of indebtedness (typically $100,000–$150,000) beyond which they will not lend any more money. School financial aid offices will have information on some popular local programs as well the major lenders who specialize in law school loans.

Law School Scholarships and Grants

Although most of the financial aid to law students comes in the form of loans, there is some help available from scholarships and grants that are based on need or merit. The sources of these handouts are quite diverse:

local bar associations and legal organizations, fraternal and religious organizations, business clubs, state agencies, veterans' organizations, and private corporations. Minority students are also eligible for additional scholarships and should investigate organizations such as the Council of Legal Education Opportunity. These funding opportunities are not easy to find. Research in local libraries, college career centers, or law school libraries is your best bet at rooting them out. These scholarships will operate on their own schedule, so it is difficult to plan around them, but they are worth the extra effort.

Law schools will also have scholarships available as part of their aid packages. The amount and extent of these funds depends on the wealth of the school. Law schools generally display these opportunities prominently in their financial aid information and disperse the money through their normal financial aid administration process. The availability of these funds is subject to the same time constraints as loan money, which should reinforce your motivation to get your financial aid information to the schools early.

LAW SCHOOL DEBT

Once you have considered your assets, investigated the costs of law school, and thought about the various sources of help in minimizing those expenses, you are likely to discover one small problem. You will probably still wind up incurring a significant amount of debt. How much debt can you or should you take on? You will have to determine your own comfort zone for the amount you will invest in your legal education. Be honest with yourself throughout this process. If you will be miserable living in a cheap apartment and scrimping on every penny and night out, then try to avoid the schools that will force you to live that way, even if that means avoiding some of the big-name institutions. Your quality of life during your legal education has an effect upon your academic performance, so do not plan to live like a hermit if you could not tolerate it.

This is a serious issue, which you should not face alone. Take advantage of professional financial and investment advice. Anyone who is going to help pay the bills, such as parents or a spouse, will want to, and should, voice an opinion. As always, talking with current law students in your financial shoes is a good starting point.

Think of your education expenses just as you would any major investment. You may be able to cover your costs at the most expensive school in the country, but is that a good use of your money? You are assuming that your future income-earning potential (perhaps enhanced by attending a more prestigious, and thus more expensive, school) will allow you to pay off the debt relatively easily. You have to consider the side effects of carrying large amounts of debt versus the benefits you can get from attending a prestigious school or not working during the school year. On the other hand, a fanatical determination to avoid any amount of debt could cost you more in the long term if you do not receive the same caliber of education you otherwise could.

Realize that the amount of debt you assume will constrain your opportunities once you graduate. Many law students decide that they will go to a better school, which will put them heavily in debt, reasoning that their increased earning power will compensate them for the short-term sacrifice. While this is the right choice for many, it has important consequences.

For one, you are almost forced to practice law after you graduate, even if you discover in the course of law school that you have no desire to do so. This is what you are qualified to do, and there are not many jobs in other fields that will pay so much so soon. Even if you do want to practice law upon graduation, your debt load may sharply curtail your career options. Only a narrow range of jobs, in the private law firm sector, are lucrative enough to allow you to live well and to make your debt payments. These jobs are hard to get precisely because of their salaries (and come at a cost to you in terms of quality of life). Virtually the entire range of public interest jobs simply do not pay well enough for you to both pay off loans and live well.

Many students who do not want to work in the private law firm environment decide to take such a job for a few years to pay off their loans and then switch over to the area in which they really want to practice. This is more difficult to do than it sounds. The lure of the golden handcuffs is difficult to resist, and many people who start at private law firms with the firm intention of returning to the public sector simply stay in the more luxurious environment.

A few schools have recognized this problem and have implemented programs of loan forgiveness (and even tuition forgiveness at one school) for graduates who take jobs in the public sector (broadly defined) for a period of years. These programs forgive some portion of school loans for graduates who work in public interest jobs and who earn less than a set amount (commonly between $25,000 and $35,000). These programs are no magic bullet, but they can be exceptionally helpful in reducing the financial sacrifice required from those who want to do public interest work. If you are interested, look closely at the details of these programs.

Once you have investigated thoroughly the three basic questions posed at the beginning of Chapter 10—Which law schools are best for me? Which law schools might accept me? Which law schools can I afford?—you should have a list of schools that meet your academic, social, and financial criteria and at which you have a chance of getting accepted. The next steps are clear: take the LSAT and start filling out applications.

13

THE LSAT

Feared by many, loved by few, the Law School Admission Test (LSAT) is the common hurdle all prospective law students must overcome. The purpose of the test is to provide law school admissions committees with an objective standard by which to judge the applicants to their school. The designers of the LSAT claim that the test accurately measures the reasoning, reading, and analytical skills that are essential to success in law school and as a lawyer. The LSAT functions as shorthand for admissions officers, condensing years of education and experience into a several-hour burst of intense mental activity. It allows the admissions people to rank all their applicants with a tool that is not supposed to be affected by differences in the test takers' academic and social backgrounds. The LSAT is also the only part of the application guaranteed to be solely the product of the individual.

On the other hand, some critics have challenged the validity of the LSAT. They dispute that the exam can truly measure the complex set of skills that lawyers require, particularly given the variety of background experiences that shape individual skills in these areas. Instead, they claim, the only thing that the LSAT measures well is how good you are at taking the LSAT. They propose that admissions committees should concentrate on the other aspects of the law school application, such as grades in college and the personal statement, which better reveal the individual applicant.

However accurate their charges, the critics remain a distinct minority. The people who really count (i.e., members of admissions committees) rely heavily on the LSAT. Your test results and your collegiate grade-point average are the only factors some schools consider in their admissions procedure. Some schools give the LSAT twice as much weight as the GPA. Even at schools that attach less importance to the

140

test scores, a low LSAT score may sink an otherwise outstanding application. Therefore, accept the fact that the LSAT is here to stay, and plan how you can use the test to your advantage.

BACKGROUND OF THE LSAT

The LSAT is a service of the Law School Admission Council. The council is made up of the 191 law schools in the United States and Canada that are approved by the American Bar Association (this covers virtually every law school in both countries). The council and its operating organization, the Law School Admission Services (Law Services), play no role in the actual admissions process of any school; they exist to assist the member schools in evaluating the applicants. The primary ways in which Law Services does this are by writing and administering the LSAT and serving as a clearinghouse of information for the schools on each person's score and academic history.

Few people see the LSAT as an opportunity to demonstrate their ability. The primary explanation for this lies in the perceived difficulty of the test. Most people feel the LSAT is not easy. They are right; the test is not meant to be easy. The LSAT is a time-pressure test. The test designers intentionally provide less time to complete each section of the test than most people would need to complete it. This can leave people with a frantic feeling that they could have done much better if only they had had a few more minutes. Another source of stress is the substantive material of the LSAT. It is meant to test ways of thinking rather than specific facts. This makes it impossible to study and master specific facts that will appear on the test. This is a dismaying proposition for many, since one of the best ways to be comfortable when taking a test is to feel that you have an excellent handle on the material.

Having duly emphasized the gloom-and-doom aspect of the LSAT, we nevertheless point out the silver lining that brightens the picture (at least a little bit). While the LSAT is undeniably important to admissions officers, and therefore to you, it is not the only factor that will be considered. If you have a high undergraduate grade-point average, it will help to compensate for a lower LSAT score. Some schools place a higher premium upon grades than on the standardized score (reasoning that the cumulative picture built by years of schooling is a better indicator than a three-hour test). On the other hand, the LSAT is also an opportunity for people who have lower GPAs to distinguish themselves by doing well.

Try to keep a sense of perspective on the difficulty of the test. Remember that you take exams throughout your entire academic career and that many of the skills you acquired for succeeding on those tests are applicable to the LSAT. This advice can be extremely difficult to follow in practice, but remember that everyone is taking the same test and that everyone will have the same problems that you have. Very few people walk out the door certain that they made no mistakes (they are probably wrong anyway). The LSAT is designed to be tough but fair. The designers screen their questions thoroughly via the "experimental" section of each test (more on this later) in order to weed out the truly impossible questions. Finally, while mastery of the subject material is not possible, there *are* ways of preparing yourself for the test that can dramatically improve your familiarity and comfort level with the LSAT. This sort of preparation is the best way, and an effective one, to ensure that your score will be the best that it can be.

FORMAT OF THE LSAT

The LSAT is a standardized test consisting of five thirty-five-minute sections of multiple-choice questions, plus one thirty-minute writing sample. While there are five sections of questions, there are only three types of questions:

- logical reasoning
- analytical reasoning
- reading comprehension

These broad categories are meant to measure your ability to perform the skills essential to success in law school. Each test presents the sections in a different order but has two sections of logical reasoning questions, one section of analytical reasoning questions, and one section of reading comprehension questions. Each section asks only one type of question. The fifth, or "experimental," section changes on every test; it can include any of the three types of questions.

Logical Reasoning

These multiple-choice questions are designed to measure your ability to analyze and criticize arguments. The designers indicate the importance of this skill for lawyers by dedicating two sections of the LSAT to this type of question. Each question presents a short passage on virtually any topic and asks you to critique an aspect of it. You might have to find a flaw or an assumption in the author's argument, draw a conclusion from the principles given in the passage, or identify the chain of reasoning within the passage. You are not expected to know the formal terms or rules of logic, although such knowledge might be useful. The passages come from a wide variety of sources, such as magazines, editorials, or even advertisements, but do not require any outside information to analyze them.

Analytical Reasoning

This section, often called the games section, is meant to measure your ability to assess a series of statements or rules and make deductions based upon this analysis. Typically, this section presents a series of related principles or facts (e.g., Brian is taller than Anton but shorter than Steve) and asks from four to seven questions about what further deductions may be made from these statements. This section usually has four such scenarios. There are different versions of logic games that frequently appear on the LSAT, but there is a common strategy to solve these puzzles. You make a diagram of the problem, encompassing the given information as completely as possible, and then apply the principles implicit in the given material to fill in the blanks. The questions are designed so the answers are independent of each other. This is done to ensure that a mistake on the first question in a set doesn't automatically mean that the rest of the problems in that set will be wrong. Unfortunately, a wrong answer to any question is often the result of a flawed analysis early in the problem, and this is likely to have unfortunate effects on other questions, despite the best intentions of the designers.

Reading Comprehension

This portion of the LSAT is familiar to everyone who has taken the SAT or the ACT test, although the passages selected are naturally more complicated and difficult than the ones used in either of those tests. The purpose of the section is to measure your ability to read and comprehend complex passages on unfamiliar subjects. The readings concern a wide range of topics—including essentially any field in the humanities or sciences, ethics, or law. Knowledge about the subject of the selection helps you comprehend the passage in less time, but the selections are intentionally made obscure enough that it would be unlikely that you would have more than a passing knowledge of the topic. One recent test included selections from the history of cytology (the study of cells); the literature of Phillis Wheatley, the Revolutionary War-era American poet; a comparison of the adversarial and inquisitorial criminal procedure systems; and a discussion on the meaning of *professional.* Even if you had written your senior honors thesis on any of those subjects, an errorless response would not be guaranteed, because the problems require analysis of the material rather than mere comprehension. Of course, if you understand the substantive aspect of the reading it obviously helps the speed and sophistication of your analysis, but the LSAT requires more.

The Experimental Section

One of the multiple-choice sections will be the mysterious experimental section. This portion of the test looks, feels, and tests like one of the other three categories but does not count in the determination of the final score. Instead, Law Services uses the results of this section as a guide for future test questions. The experimental section is not labeled as such and may be the first set of problems, or the fifth, or anywhere in between. This keeps test takers in the dark as to which are the sections of the test that count. This preserves the scientific integrity of the experimental section by ensuring that everyone will make a whole-hearted effort to solve the problems. Essentially, Law Services forces everyone who takes the LSAT to serve as a guinea pig for future exams. While you may feel that this is undesirable and stressful (do you really want to struggle for an extra thirty-five minutes serving the whims of the LSAT gods?), the usefulness of the experimental section to the designers of the LSAT ensures that it will remain.

The main problem with the experimental section, other than the annoyance factor, is that it may be more difficult than the average section because it hasn't been tried out yet. This makes it more likely that you will have a difficult time with this portion of the test. In itself this doesn't hurt, since the experimental section isn't included in your final score, but doing poorly on one section, or even feeling that you have done poorly on one section, can have negative consequences on your attitude and performance for the rest of the test. It is essential, therefore, to remember the strong possibility that any section that seems exceptionally difficult may be the harmless experimental section. In fact, it is best to assume that this is the case and proceed as if a poor performance on that particular part has no effect on your score.

After you have finished the test, you may want to check to see whether that assumption was correct. The first step is simple—check which category of problems had an extra section. If there is more than one reading comprehension section, then one of them is experimental. Narrowing down the choice further requires conferring with other people who took the test on the same date. Law Services gives different experimental sections to people who are taking what is otherwise the same test at the same location. Therefore, asking around is likely to reveal what parts of a particular LSAT everybody shared and what parts were not shared. The unshared sections must be experimental. The order in which the sections are presented varies from test to test, so you will have to recall specific problems within the sections in order to compare. This approach works better for the reading comprehension and analytical reasoning sections because they are easier to remember, but is certainly possible for logical reasoning.

If the section that you were worried about turns out to be the experimental section, then you can relax; it won't hurt your result. Unfortunately, doing well on a experimental section, even a horrendously difficult one, doesn't help you at all (remember you are just a guinea pig). If you discover that the section you were worried about is not experimental, you may want to cancel your test. The pros and cons of this strategy are discussed later in this chapter.

The Writing Sample

The final stage in the LSAT inflicts much less mental stress on most test takers. The thirty-minute writing sample reflects an effort by the makers of the LSAT to assess your writing skills. The essay you will be invited to write will be extremely broad and will require no prior knowledge to complete. It is a version of the standard collegiate essay exam. A typical question presents a short hypothetical situation that gives you two conflicting principles to resolve. For example, a town interested in both commercial development and in retaining its small-town character asks you to decide what kind of building it should build in a vacant lot. You would be given two choices that partly satisfy each requirement and asked to recommend one. There is no right or wrong answer on this type of test, as either choice can be supported logically. As a general rule, choose the option that seems to give more room for discussion, but be careful to include the pros and the cons of both in your essay.

Since there cannot be a right or wrong answer, your response is not corrected or included in your LSAT score. Instead, photocopies of the writing sample accompany the report of your scores that the law schools receive. This provides the schools with an example of how you write in a situation in which you don't have the time to polish your prose as you do in the personal statement and the other documents you might submit in your application. The importance of writing ability for law students is undeniable. It is questionable whether the writing sample is a meaningful indication of your writing skills, but Law Services keeps this section in order to placate critics who charge that a multiple-choice format is a poor way to gauge the thinking and analytical abilities the LSAT attempts to measure. Law schools vary in how much attention, if any, they give to the writing sample. You shouldn't assume that your effort will not be scrutinized by an eagle-eyed admissions committee member, so give it a legitimate try, but don't agonize if you don't feel that you set a new standard for argumentative essay writing. The writing sample is unlikely to make or break your application.

LSAT Scores

Your score for the test, not your writing sample, will attract the attention of admissions officers. The scores range from 120 to 180 with the average at 150. The higher the score, the better. The test scores form a bell curve, so only the very top test takers get scores in the 170s and only the very lowest are in the 120s. Your score is based on the number of questions you answer correctly, so there is no penalty for wrong answers (as there is in the SAT). Each test is scored differently to reflect its difficulty, but there is not much variation between each test, so a 160 on one test will equal a 160 on another. As we discussed in Chapter 11, your score on the LSAT is without question the single most important factor in determining your chances of getting into law school.

WHEN TO TAKE THE LSAT

The LSAT is given four times a year, usually in June, October, December, and February. The mechanics of signing up for the test are pretty simple. First, get the current LSAT registration book. It is available at undergraduate career centers or from Law Services directly. The address of Law Services is listed in Appendix B. Law Services also maintains an automated telephone service where you can ask for general information and additional materials. The registration book gives the precise test dates and the deadlines for registration. Regular registration currently costs $76 and ends about a month before the test date; registering later costs an extra $44 but gives you an extra two weeks to make up your mind. The book also gives a detailed list of where the test is given for which test dates—not every site is available for all four dates. Another reason to register sooner rather than waiting for the deadline for any given test is that the test centers fill up and you may not get your first, or even second, choice. The inconvenience of traveling to Spearfish, South Dakota (yes, it's given there), would not only aggravate you but add the stress of finding the test center to the stress from the test itself. Avoid this; register early.

Reasons to Take the Test Early

There are many important considerations you should ponder before deciding which LSAT date you want. There are three powerful reasons to try and take the LSAT very early in the application process.

1. *Knowing your LSAT score helps you decide which schools you should consider most seriously.* Ideally, you should know your

score on the LSAT before you begin the application process. The combination of your GPA and your LSAT score provides a good indicator of the law schools at which you are likely to be accepted, the schools at which you might be accepted, and the schools at which you would be a long shot. This knowledge simplifies your application process (and saves some application fees) by reducing the number of schools to which you will apply. Remember that it takes Law Services about six weeks after the test date to report your score, so even taking the October test (if you are applying for the next year's class) will not leave much time to narrow the range of possible schools. Your scores on simulated or old LSATs will give you an idea of what you can expect, but they are not good substitutes for the real thing.

2. *Taking the LSAT early allows you to apply to law schools early.* This strategy, covered in greater detail in Chapter 14, may increase your odds of acceptance, particularly at schools that fill slots as they read through their applicants' materials. This is true to some degree even if the school doesn't officially practice rolling admissions. You do not want the lag time between when you take the test and when Law Services reports your score to the law schools to hurt your chances of admission. Waiting until the December test can only hurt you (the February test is too late for most schools' admission deadlines).

3. *An early date preserves the possibility of retaking the LSAT.* Ideally, the issue will not arise, but you may want to cancel your test before it is scored or be thoroughly unhappy with it once you receive your score. While there are some reasons not to retake the LSAT, you want to have the option. Do not tie your hands by delaying until you can't try again. Even people who choose the October test may find themselves in a time bind, since they then have to rely on the December test for a retake. This possibility is the best reason to choose either the February or the June date.

Reasons to Wait Before Taking the LSAT

After stressing the rationale behind taking the test as soon as possible (and our preference for that strategy), it is important to note some reasons why you *shouldn't* rush out and take the next test. One fundamental criterion you should consider is your own intellectual development. The test is designed to challenge college graduates. The more academic experience you have, the better you are likely to do. It makes sense to proceed as far along your learning curve as possible, so taking the test much before your senior year is probably counterproductive.

You must also consider the amount of time you will have to study for the LSAT. You need at least a month to prepare prior to the test. Do you have the necessary hours? Take a realistic look at how much free time you will have. Don't try to graduate, star on your collegiate fencing team, find a new job, and study for the LSAT simultaneously. Figure out the best window of opportunity, and make a schedule in which LSAT studying is your first priority. The payoff in terms of peace of mind and test performance will make this commitment worthwhile. If there is more than one potential window, as there often is, it is safer to go with the earlier option. This prevents an unforeseeable accident or emergency from foreclosing your ability to get ready.

Finally, remember that many test sites do not give the LSAT on all the dates. Most are open for the October and December rounds but not necessarily for the other two. If only one center is convenient, you may have little choice. This is one situation in which traveling to a further site may be worth the extra trouble, time, and expense. After all, Spearfish, South Dakota, may be beautiful in the spring.

Those of you who do not plan to apply to law schools for the next year are well positioned to avoid the time pressures that plague those on a tighter schedule. You have the luxury of picking the optimum time to study for and to take the test without the concern about having time to cancel or retake the test. LSAT scores remain valid for three years, so it is quite possible to take the LSAT well before you anticipate applying.

PREPARING FOR THE LSAT

It is important to understand that the LSAT measures your reasoning and analytical abilities. It is even more important to understand what the LSAT does *not* measure. It does not claim to reveal your knowledge of the law or any other background information you might study. This has an extremely practical consequence. You should not attempt frantically to stuff your brain with information in the weeks leading up to test, even if this worked amazingly well in college. It will simply depress you. Preparation is essential, but it is familiarity with the style and pacing of the test that is key, not factual knowledge. At some level, you will either get it or you won't. There is only so much that you can add to a lifetime of accumulated mental conditioning (i.e., your reasoning and analytical abilities) by practicing and reviewing for a month or two. This should not be an excuse for a lackluster effort at preparation ("It's all genetics anyway"). Proper preparation will make you calmer, more efficient, and ready to think the way the LSAT demands. This leads directly to higher LSAT scores.

There are two mainstream methods of studying for the LSAT:

- independent study
- commercial preparatory courses

There are common elements between them, and a combination of the two is also possible. They are two paths to the same goal, and you will have to decide for yourself which will work best for you. This requires a pretty simple exercise in self-assessment. The basic question you must ask yourself is whether you have the self-discipline to put in the necessary hours by yourself or whether you would find a mixture of stick and carrot really helpful in completing the same amount of work. Each approach has accompanying advantages and disadvantages, but this is the central question that divides the two paths.

Independent Study

Independent study, as the name implies, means that you devote yourself to a program of self-learning rather than relying on others to teach you the same material. Of course, independent study is not truly independent, unless you meditate in a darkened room awaiting a visitation by the LSAT-knowledge fairy. You will use a variety of tools and study aids, possibly including those published by the same companies that market and run the prep courses. Independent studying is also not studying, at least not in the manner for which college has prepared you. You are honing and sharpening your faculties, not learning a new language or memorizing dates.

If you choose independent study, your first decision is when you should start your work. Naturally, this depends on the intensity of your study plan. You might practice an average of two hours a day starting six weeks before D-day, or you could try to cram six hours a day for two weeks. The former is a decidedly better approach. While this is the standard line on studying for any test, it is absolutely essential for the LSAT. Remember that the goal is not knowledge but a facility with taking the test and thinking the way the designers want. This entails a building-block learning process that you simply cannot condense effectively. You need to familiarize yourself with the style, speed, and format of the test. This requires repeated practice exams and exercises. If you don't concentrate while you practice, you don't get much benefit from the work. Total focus on the problems, which should be your goal, is not sustainable for longer than a few hours. After this point there are diminishing returns, as you make more mistakes, react more slowly, and retain less. Taking three practice tests on the day before the real one will teach you little and create enormous stress. Avoid this devastating combination.

It is also safer to start earlier if you plan on doing it on your own. You may find yourself struggling to understand the concepts or unable to make yourself work. A two-month lead time allows two or three weeks to discover that the independent approach is not the best for you and still gives you enough time to seek refuge in a prep course.

How to Prepare by Yourself

So, how do you prepare on your own? As noted, there is no body of facts you can master by brute memorization. Your real goal is to become better at taking the LSAT. The best plan of attack involves constantly placing yourself in the situation you will be in when you take the real thing. Take as many simulated tests as you can, and make them as close to the real thing in terms of the time you allow yourself, your concentration, and your background environment.

Most people find the LSAT, particularly the logical reasoning and analytical reasoning sections, unlike any test they have taken before. The thinking skills the LSAT seeks to measure are different but not necessarily difficult. Constant repetition will teach you to think as the LSAT demands. Unprepared people who take the test may be perfectly capable of answering every question correctly, but they won't get the chance—the test moves too quickly for them to figure out approaches to each question during the test. Since the LSAT has a limited number of types of questions that reappear on each test in slightly different forms, a prior exposure to the LSAT format greatly facilitates your ability to analyze the issues correctly. You won't be familiar with any given question on the actual day, but you should have done several problems that are similar enough that your brain has a head start on tackling them.

Repeated simulations will also reduce your anxiety level when you actually get to the test site and allow you to focus on solving the problems. Being calm is particularly important for the LSAT. The whole point of the test is to measure your ability to think and reason clearly; you must be in control to do this well. On a purely pragmatic level, the minutes and seconds you spend in a state of panic are lost. You cannot afford this on the LSAT; there is not enough time as it is.

Practice Materials

Obviously, to simulate tests you will need some practice materials. Without question, the best studying materials are the LSAT tests from previous years that Law Services makes available. No other simulated tests and exercises are going to be as authentic or challenging or well written as the real thing. Law Services will give you one version for free. You can pick it up when you get the registration book or request it from Law Services. Other previous exams are available at a relatively small price.

There may be enough material there to satisfy your studying needs, but if not, you can turn to the numerous books published by the LSAT review companies or other LSAT "experts." Law Services also has its own line of study aids apart from the actual tests. These volumes provide a virtually unlimited supply of exercises. The primary advantage of these outside sources is that they provide a framework and strategies with which to approach the LSAT in far more detail than this book attempts. Most of this is common sense, but it is not mentioned either in the minimal instructions in the LSAT registration book or in the tests themselves. You may find it difficult to choose among the competing experts. Since you can't beat the LSAT, in practice there probably isn't much difference between their strategies. Go to a bookstore or to your undergraduate career center and page through a couple of the contenders. Take the one that makes the most sense to you.

The other benefit of these guides is that they will often provide explanations for the answers to their exercises. Since the LSAT asks for the best answer, not the only answer, questions will often have more than one potentially correct answer. If all you have is an answer key, you may not understand why the answer LSAT wanted is better than your response. To avoid mistakes, you want to understand the rationale behind the question.

However, the simulated exams and exercises are not the real thing. Their major flaw is that they are generally not as well written or as difficult as the LSAT. This makes sense. Law Services devotes more time and energy to making the product then the other experts devote to imitating it. As noted, Law Services also has the luxury of trying out experimental sections on each exam. As a consequence, you may become frustrated with muddled and unclear sample questions in the other books. Even the versions that explain the answers to their simulated tests do not necessarily correct for this problem.

In summary, the review books are useful to the extent that they give you an overall scheme for taking the LSAT. They also provide supplemental study material and explanations. Don't expect a magical formula that will by itself give you ten points. A good plan would be to start off using these guides to familiarize yourself with the basic ideas and strategies, and then apply these lessons to the practice LSAT tests as the date approaches.

Practice Test Taking

As a general rule, keep your practice conditions as close to live test conditions as possible. Timing yourself is absolutely critical. You need to understand the pacing that is best for you prior to the test, and this only comes about through practicing each section at thirty-five minutes. You may want to relax this rule during your first few attempts at each section, but the sooner that you force yourself to conform to the time constraints, the better. The temptation always exists to give yourself just a minute or two more. Be virtuous and resist. You will probably want to begin by doing one section and then taking a break and reviewing the answers. Try to build up your endurance by gradually extending the number of sections you do without a break. The LSAT is a grueling test; you need to mentally condition yourself just as an athlete does. Otherwise you will hit the fifth section with the energy of a couch potato, and your score will reflect this state of mind.

You should apply the same idea to the study environment. You don't need to check into the nearest monastery, but try to limit the intrusions of daily life, particularly the phone, while you are practicing. You want to concentrate and work on your pacing; your roommate's social life will probably not be on the test. You may want to practice at the same hour that you will take the test, particularly in the week leading up to it. Morning tests are the norm; if you are not a morning person, you may need the rude wake-up call of morning practice sessions to ensure that you are not half-conscious when it counts.

Commercial Preparatory Courses

You may decide that you would rather be taught than teach yourself. The preparatory courses offered by private companies and universities may fill that role for you. Be forewarned, you will not merely sit at the feet of the wise old Buddha lapping up pearls of test-taking wisdom. You should work as hard in a commercial course as you would if you followed the independent study program, if not harder.

There are a variety of commercial possibilities, depending on where you live. The major players, such as Kaplan or Princeton Review, compete with numerous smaller operators ranging from former law students doing private tutoring to university-sponsored classes. The programs differ in terms of cost, classroom hours, and the resources they make available. The typical program offers twenty to forty hours of classroom time and supplementary practice devices ranging from tapes to tests to study labs. Tutors will give advice, examples, and reassurance. You will be thoroughly drilled in the particular test-taking strategy that this program follows.

A major benefit of the programs is the discipline they impose. By providing a structured framework and the monetary incentive (after all, you don't want to waste your fee), the courses make it significantly easier to put in the unexciting but necessary hours. This is more than half the battle of LSAT preparation, so even if the course does nothing more for you, it may be worth your while. The course will ensure that you drill on simulated exercises that approximate test conditions.

Naturally, the programs are designed to do much more than merely goading you into working hard. People who have trouble understanding the substance of the LSAT or who want help with test-taking strategies may find the classroom time invaluable. The instructors will walk through the practice tests and explain the options, the reasons behind the right answer, and mistakes that many people make. Since the LSAT repeats different versions of the same problems, this may be of significant help. One wild card is that the value of the classroom time depends heavily on the quality of the tutor. Ask around to determine the reputation of any particular program before you commit to it.

A final benefit you may derive from participating in a class is the feeling of psychological calm that comes when you have done everything you could have done to prepare. You don't want to look around the room as the LSAT tests are distributed and feel as if everyone else knows the secret way to success and you don't. This feeling may not be entirely rational, but it can seem quite real. You buy a security blanket when you take a preparatory class and see others struggling just as you are.

One last point touches on a disadvantage, perhaps the only one, of taking a prep course: the cost. You may pay over $700 for the privilege of slaving away in drill sessions. Even less extensive or less prestigious programs will charge hundreds of dollars. If the money is no problem, then you might as well do it; it can't hurt and might be extremely helpful.

If you are also among the majority of people who feel that $700 is a significant amount of money to throw around, you will have to think harder about whether to take a course. First, be an informed consumer. Ask friends who have taken local courses what their experience was, and look at the materials they received. Be wary of guarantees of improved scores. Virtually everyone will improve simply by taking the test repeatedly.

Second, remember the main advantages you derive from the course: discipline, psychological calm, and instruction. Assess for yourself how much you alone can adequately provide each element. Discipline you can supply yourself (Or can you? It's tougher than you think). The importance of psychological calm is highly variable. It is probably a relatively minor consideration for most people. It is the value of the instruction and the likelihood (or not) of replacing it with self-study that is so difficult to judge.

You have to assess your own capabilities honestly. Resist the herd instinct. The core of what is taught in the classes is available in published books. The test-taking tips and strategies are not incredibly complicated, but they may not be communicated as well in print as they would be in person from a knowledgeable instructor. How good are you at self-instruction?

The value of these tips and strategies to you is another issue. In part, it depends on what score you are seeking. What is your target score? If you are shooting for the highest scores, you will probably find the suggestion that you guess on numerous questions (a common tactic) ridiculous. If you aren't, this strategy may make a great deal of sense, since it allows you to spend more time on the questions you are more likely to answer correctly. The best way to get a rough assessment of your capabilities is to try by yourself first. Take the free copy of the old LSAT test and then decide.

Finally, you have to recognize that while $700 is serious money to most of us, it pales in comparison with the cost of your legal education. This may run over $100,000 at the more expensive schools. Given the importance of the LSAT to your application, it may make sense to invest funds earlier in the process to ensure that your really big-ticket expenditure, that is, your tuition, goes to the best place possible for you.

In the end, this is a very personal decision. Harry and Chris took opposite approaches to preparing for the LSAT, and both ended up quite pleased with how well they were prepared. Harry took a commercial preparatory class. He found the class particularly helpful, in part because it helped him remember, after several years away from school, how to take standardized tests. It greatly helped Harry understand the basic mind-set of the LSAT questions, and he saw it as money well spent. Chris, on the other hand, studied independently for the LSAT. The high price of review classes was a major reason that Chris decided to go it alone. He felt that he was self-disciplined enough to devote the necessary time to the test, and he judged he was not then making enough money to justify spending that much of his income on a review class.

TEST-TAKING TIPS

Finally, the day of the big test draws near. The day before the LSAT should be much like the day before any major exam. What worked for you before? If you prefer to relax the day before, do it. It's equally acceptable to review one last time; just don't spend so much time on it that you feel absolutely wiped out and ill at the prospect of another three hours the next day. The most valuable thing you may do to prepare for the LSAT the day before may be ensuring that you are on the right sleep cycle for the hour of the test. The day before the test should not be spent taking three full simulations in a frantic attempt to catch up on all the work you intended to do but somehow did not. If you are that unprepared, you shouldn't take the test anyway. Accept the monetary loss and resolve to do better next time.

General common sense recommendations apply as well to the day of the test. Get to the exam center early enough that you can calmly register. Bring the required materials, particularly your admission ticket. Bring a sufficient number of sharpened pencils and a watch. Since the test can last as long as six or seven hours, including the registration, organization, and distribution of the forms, you may want to bring some food or drink. Some test proctors don't allow this, but it doesn't hurt to try. If they take it away, grin and bear it.

There are also several important test-taking practices specific to the LSAT that you should remember:

- Answer every question.
- Use all the time available.
- Read the test carefully.

Answer Every Question

There are five choices for each question, but there is no penalty for wrong answers, so you might as well take the 20 percent chance at winning the lottery on every question. Some people find it more efficient to attempt every question seriously, whereas others find that guessing on some questions allows them the time to get more answers correct overall. Know which tactic you will follow before you begin. Pace yourself so that whatever strategy you follow has a chance to work. Remember that the LSAT, unlike the SAT, doesn't make the questions more challenging as the test progresses. The first question is designed to be as easy or as difficult as the last. Don't get flustered if you have trouble early; just keep focused on the section until time is up.

Use All the Time Available

Don't plan on returning to a section to complete a portion that troubled you. LSAT forbids this. In the unlikely case that you have time left at the end of a section, check your answers for that section. One simple way to increase the time available is to familiarize yourself with the instructions to each section when you prepare. Not only is there little information in these passages but the passages remain the same from year to year. Don't waste precious minutes "discovering" the instructions that you ignored through countless practice rounds.

Read the Test Carefully

Careful reading of the actual problems, on the other hand, is important and worth taking the time to do. A proper interpretation of the question saves time in the long run because of the nature of the test. Remember the LSAT asks for the best answer, not the only answer, and provides several possibilities that aren't wrong, just less correct than the desired response. Distinguishing among these options requires a correct interpretation of the initial question.

We will not try to provide strategies specific to each section. There are many theories out there, and it is a very individual affair as to which theory works best for you. Keep your mind open and try them on practice exercises. Stick with the ones that seem to help you. Don't allow a book or an instructor to force one approach down your throat if it doesn't work for you. There are many paths to a common end on the LSAT; search around until you find the best one for you.

POST-TEST OPTIONS

You walk out of the test center. In the best of all possible worlds, you do a small victory dance, confident that you demolished the test and sent the designers scurrying to find trickier phrasing and more subtle nuances for the next batch of unfortunates. More realistically, you want to feel that your performance accurately reflected your potential. This doesn't mean that you have to believe you answered every question correctly. You should feel confident about your answers to approximately the same number of questions as you would after a successful practice test. Not knowing your actual score produces some agony, but there are compelling reasons to accept your performance, anticipated lumps and all.

If you are concerned that you did poorly, you have two options: you may cancel your test results before you see them, or you may wait to see your scores and try again if they are too low. There are advantages and disadvantages to each approach.

Canceling Your Test Scores

Law Services gives you the option of canceling your score at the conclusion of the test; all you have to do is fill out a portion of the answer sheet. You may also cancel your score up to five days after you complete the test by contacting Law Services. Law Services regards a cancellation as irreversible, so if you have any uncertainty, you should use the five days to think about the decision.

The advantage to canceling your test is that Law Services will not give your results to the law schools. Their report will show that you canceled a test (since exposure to actual test conditions may give you a small advantage on future tests) but nothing more. Once Law Services has graded your effort, the law schools will see that grade. Law Services reports all your scores; a poor one will not be suppressed.

An obvious disadvantage of canceling prior to seeing the outcome is that you may have done perfectly well. Your emotions immediately after finishing may prevent you from rationally assessing the situation and your performance. Unless you feel that the root cause of your poor attempt was something that won't affect later efforts (you hadn't prepared adequately, you were sick, you were distracted by a personal crisis, you forgot your lucky pencil), you could emerge the second time with exactly the same doubts. You face another round of preparation, with all its attendant stress, constraints on your time, and expense. Law Services will not refund your fee or give you another try even if you cancel before they process your test. The second attempt will require less work, but a significant refresher course will be necessary.

Our suggestion is to cancel your scores only if you are absolutely convinced that you did appreciably worse than you should have. This assumes you have the option of taking a later test with no negative effects on your chances of admission. If you cannot afford to try again because of scheduling delays, consider whether you really have to apply for the next year. Time off is often a blessing in any case, regardless of the reasons that prompt it.

Problems That Were Not Your Fault

On rare occasions Law Services acknowledges that it made a mistake with the choice of test site or in the administration of the test. If the testing center was inadequate or the administrators of the test did a horrible job, Law Services may allow you another chance to take the test without reporting your score. This doesn't require that someone was using a jackhammer right outside the window where you were working, although this would certainly be grounds for a legitimate complaint. More mundane disturbing events, like an incredibly lengthy intake and test distribution process, may be sufficient for Law Services to recognize that a problem existed. If you feel that you have a complaint, you should send a letter detailing the problems to Law Services and encourage anyone else you know who took the test at that center to do the same.

If enough people report legitimate complaints, Law Services may give everyone at that site the option of retaking the test for free or including an explanatory note with your law school report explaining that the test conditions were not adequate. This process will take longer than five days to work out with Law Services, so don't depend on this in lieu of canceling your scores. You won't know your results when you make the decision, but there is that small chance. Don't deluge Law Services with trivial complaints, but a note can't hurt if you had a problem.

Taking the LSAT Again

In itself, the Law Services report with all your results would not hurt if the law school admissions committees disregarded anything other than your best effort. College admissions officers pay little attention to any SAT or ACT scores other than your best ones. Unfortunately, life gets tougher as you get older. Law schools are less forgiving than colleges in their treatment of your standardized tests. They generally take the position that LSAT scores are forever.

Law schools adopt a variety of policies that effectively wipe out the advantages of taking the LSAT a second time. There is no consistent approach; different institutions do different things. A minority of institutions will accept your highest score. If you know your target schools, you can try to establish what their policies are, either by contacting the admissions office or by consulting reference works. Your undergraduate career center may have a list of which policy each school follows.

While the policies may differ, the effects of those policies remain the same: taking the test a second time is unlikely to significantly improve your chances of admission. Law schools will often average your scores. This means you will have to improve significantly on your second attempt to make a real difference in your score. If you expected a 160 and got a 155, you will have to decide two things. First, can you really expect to get a 165? Second, is a marginal gain of two or three points on the LSAT (your gain if you actually get a 160 on the second one) worth the risk that you will not improve at all, or even do worse? Some schools might accept the second score, but knock a few points off it, which has the same effect.

These policies seem unfair. Why don't law schools take a kinder, gentler attitude toward people who don't quite get it right the first time? If the LSAT measures the skills essential for law students, then shouldn't your best score be the determining factor? The answers to these questions are less than compelling. One reason is that, on average, people who retake the test will see their scores improve slightly. Familiarity with the test helps. Law schools recognize this and discount your improvement accordingly. They do not want to encourage everyone to keep trying until they get better scores. It is inefficient for the applicants and doesn't say as much about their ability. In addition, the law school spirit is that you should take tests once and do it right. Law school courses, which depend heavily on final exams for the overall grade, reward people with this ability. Accordingly, admissions officers seek people who show the same performance skills.

You do have some options if you are decidedly unhappy with your reported score. If you are positive that you can easily surpass your previous attempt, and you won't hurt yourself by taking a later test, then retake it. One route would be to take the LSAT again, assess how you feel right after the second test, and then cancel your score if you do not feel good about your second performance. You might also use the personal statement portion of your application to explain extenuating factors that prevented you from doing your best at test time. Don't do this unless you can offer compelling reasons, such as serious illness or a personal crisis. Keep your explanation short. It's equally effective, doesn't bore the reader, and takes less space. While you want the law school to know your excuse, you don't want to sacrifice your opportunity to make your personal statement as interesting and distinctive as possible.

In the end, you receive a score between 120 and 180 (hopefully above 120, since you get that for signing your name). Your LSAT score is the last piece of the puzzle you should need to make your final decision on where to apply to law school. The next stage is the application process itself.

14

THE LAW SCHOOL
APPLICATION

Now the real fun begins. You can experience the same joy you felt when you waded through your college applications. A true return to Nirvana. Actually, the law school application is less painful in several ways. You do not have to write a different tortuous essay for each school. The factors that lead the law schools to lean heavily upon standardized scores and transcripts (not enough people to read too many applications) also work to minimize the amount of paper that you will have to send. After all, law schools have no desire to make you slave over essays they are not going to read.

WHEN TO START THE
APPLICATION PROCESS

Most law schools have application deadlines in the spring (usually from February 1 to April 1) for the following fall's entering class. Your first deadline is the most important, because once you have done the work for one application, you will have done most of the necessary work for all of them. A quick scan of your prospective schools will give you a target day toward which to work. Most schools begin accepting applications for the fall in the fall of the previous year, usually in October, although a few programs with separate application schedules accept students for summer programs or mid-year admission.

Reasons to Start Early

Usually, the sooner you start, the better. A proactive attitude in the fall is vastly preferable to looking at things three weeks prior to the deadline. While this kind of sanctimonious advice often falls on deaf ears, finishing the applications early has significant benefits other than the deep inner satisfaction of having finished the wretched process.

First, there are all sorts of deadlines during the law school application process. The LSAT registration and test dates are obvious, but many structural and logistical deadlines and delays become apparent only after you immerse yourself in the process. Writing away for applications, assembling the six or seven documents you need from five different sources, allowing your recommenders a week or two to get around to your recommendation, painstakingly typewriting your information onto the forms, and getting to the post office drains away time that you may not have budgeted. An early start also guards against the inevitable last-minute emergency, such as when a key recommender unexpectedly leaves the country for a week.

Second, and most important, you gain an advantage in the admissions race at many schools if they receive your completed materials earlier in their application cycle. This is a result of the way in which law schools process their applications. Some schools wait until all the applications are in before starting to work through the files, so applications mailed the day of the deadline are not penalized. However, many schools promote administrative efficiency by using rolling admissions, i.e., decisions are made on files as they come across the door. Admissions officers have a sense of the caliber of candidate that will be accepted. Clear acceptances and rejections can be dealt with summarily (increasing the odds that good candidates will pick this school), and the close calls will be held until the quality of the application class becomes clearer.

Early applicants enjoy several advantages under the rolling admissions scheme. Admissions officers are under less time pressure and may not yet feel the crush of hundreds of unread folders when they pick up your carefully crafted package. Any psychological boost you can get in this highly subjective procedure is a plus. Furthermore, if you apply late, the school may have accepted as many people as it possibly can, or it may be down to the last few slots, which it will fill with only truly extraordinary candidates. You might be wildly overqualified, but if all the slots are filled, everyone loses except the less qualified person who applied earlier and got your spot. Applying early may not get you into a school that otherwise would not take you, but applying late may cost you a spot at a school that otherwise would love to have you.

Reasons to Delay Your Applications

There are a few reasons why you might want to delay your applications, but they are less compelling as a rule than the arguments to start early. The best reason to wait is that you want to get your LSAT score before you apply so you can accurately gauge the strength of your application. Of course, now that you have received the gospel that you should take the LSAT early, this should not be a problem. If you read this book too late to help you with that little detail, this is a quandary. In sending out applications before you know your LSAT score, you balance the possibility of guessing wrong on your score against the advantage of finishing the applications early. If you can afford to send out an extra round of applications if it turns out that you did significantly better or worse than you expected, go ahead and gamble and send out the first ones. The advantage is worth the potential expense. At the least, prepare as much of the material as you can before you find out your scores so you can move immediately.

Other common excuses for delay are, in our view, less valid. You may want to wait until an event, competition, or other accomplishment or experience happens so you can include it in your biographical section or write about it on your personal statement. This is probably a poor exchange. There are very few outside experiences that are going to be so impressive that they will boost you above your compatriots. If you plan on doing something truly monumental, you can supplement your application packet at a later date, or tell the law school what you anticipate will happen. Chris found this particular excuse particularly appealing because it allowed him to delay working on his applications under the justification that he was actually improving his chances by waiting. When a hoped-for internship failed to materialize, the only thing this strategy yielded was a late round of applications.

Never delay solely because you are waiting for more information or a visit to the school. You should have done the investigation in the summer or early fall, but even if you have not, you should be able to pick out at least some of your choices with a bare minimum of research. At least start with those before letting your agonizing choice between State U and the U of State drag down the rest of your applications.

HOW MANY APPLICATIONS YOU SHOULD COMPLETE

The culmination of all your research comes when you decide on the schools that will be the lucky recipients of your life story and application fee. You will want to pare down the list to a finite number, but what is that number? The answer, of course, is, it depends. The typical applicant applies to four or five schools, but there are good reasons to deviate from the average.

The limits on your ability to apply to as many schools as you want are your time and patience for filling out forms and your ability to write out application checks. No admissions officer cares how many places you apply to. Application fees, however, are a real limit. They have crept up to $60 at some schools, and they are nonrefundable. They don't even go toward your tuition if you enroll. But it is also important for you to place these fees in context. These fees are a small investment compared to the thousands you will spend on your education, so do not go overboard trying to determine the bare minimum of schools. Ask yourself how badly you want to go to law school next year. If your heart is not set on going to law school immediately, you can be more selective, since you can always try again. In this scenario you can afford to apply to only the few schools at the top of your list.

If you are sure that you want to start law school immediately, then you need to apply to schools throughout your likely range of acceptance. Use the three basic categories that many people have used for sending out college applications. Divide the schools into those at which you are a long shot, those at which you are competitive, and those at which you are virtually a sure thing. As discussed in Chapter 11, your LSAT score and your undergraduate grade-point average are your basic reference points for your chances of acceptance (with some small modifications depending upon your background and experience). Use the

LSAT/GPA grids in the law school guides to translate your scores into rough percentages. If you have to make this decision before you know your LSAT score (take the test early!), you will have to make an educated guess. If this is the situation, it makes sense to apply to a few extra schools at both ends of the spectrum.

Some people will not have safety schools, and applicants interested in the best schools will find there is no such thing as a sure bet in the top ten, but most people will have schools in all three categories. The next step is to apportion your applications among the categories. The bulk of your applications should be to schools where you are a competitive candidate. If you apply to three or four of these schools, the odds suggest that at least one application will be successful. Choosing one or two safety schools and one or two long-shot schools then covers the bases and protects you somewhat from the uncertainties of the law school application process.

AN APPLICATION OVERVIEW

The first step in filling out the forms (acquiring the applications) is easy. They are available from a variety of sources—from university career centers, law school fairs, and the schools themselves. The LSAT registration book has some nifty premade request forms and the addresses. Or, design your own, and send them out to every school you can dream of attending. It is an easy and cheap way to get information and to fill your mailbox in those slow months before the holidays.

Imagine that your labors have finally paid off, you have chosen the perfect mix of schools, and you have their applications sitting in front of you. Now the fun begins in earnest as you open the glossy and enticing packages.

The basic components of the application do not change from school to school. The requirements include:

- a personal statement
- biographical data
- undergraduate and graduate (if any) transcripts
- LSAT score
- letters of recommendation

This entails significant logistical work, but usually you will only need to slave over one essay and all the completed forms will only fill a few pages.

How to Make Your Application Stand Out

The downside of this uniform application format is that it makes each element of the application much more important and makes it harder to distinguish yourself from the rest of the pack. Separating yourself from the mob is the hallmark of a good application. There are some general practices that will help you do this.

Complete the Application

In large part, this means that you must devote enough time to the application forms to do them right. Writing, editing, rewriting, and passing around your personal statement can easily take weeks. Frivolous applications are easy to reject.

Check Your Spelling

Grammatical mistakes, typos, missing letters, or misspellings in any of your submissions send the wrong signal.

Make Your Forms as Neat as Possible

Use a typewriter or a word processor instead of relying upon your handwriting.

Follow the Guidelines on Length or Attaching Extra Pages

These format issues may have no effect on the substance of your application, but a sloppy submission sends the message that you do not care about the application or, by extension, the school. These details are even more important for your personal statement, but the lesson applies to the entire package.

Proofread Everything That Gets Mailed

Ideally, have someone else do the proofreading. By the time you finish your application you are likely to be so sick of the whole thing that you will not have the requisite amount of attention. Draft a friend or relative for the task.

View the Application as a Whole

You are trying to dazzle the admissions people with the complexity of your personality and accomplishments in a small and rigid amount of space. To do this, you have to use all the elements of the application effectively and efficiently. The personal statement is the most prominent forum for self-expression, but every element from the way you describe your extracurricular activities or work experience to the things your recommenders write about you should complement and build upon the others as much as possible. You do not want to repeat everything three times or leave out something crucial. Most important, you do not want to have inconsistencies. If you emphasize in your personal statement how much you love helping homeless people, make sure there is evidence of this interest in your supporting materials. This does not mean that every thought or feeling you mention in your statement must be extensively supported and footnoted, but make sure that your major themes bear up under scrutiny.

Getting It All Together

The coordination of all the elements of the application is much of the challenge. You must ensure that your recommendations from three or four different sources, your LSAT scores and transcripts, your biographical material, and all your financial aid information make it to the appropriate recipient (the target school, the LSDAS, the financial aid office, or the federal government). There are different deadlines for the different recipients, and it will take different amounts of time to coax each element from the respective source. The convoluted nature of the materials reflects the potential logistical confusion you may face. Some law schools try to help with the administrative details by letting you know when your application file is complete. Take advantage of the limited logistical hand-holding available, but remember that *you* bear the ultimate responsibility of making sure your file is complete. In short, you must impose some kind of organization on the process, or things will get lost.

One of the most effective ways to create order out of chaos is to make a chart that tracks the various tasks, when you must begin them, and when they must be completed. Such a chart is an opportunity for the mildly obsessive-compulsive among us to indulge in an exquisite creation of detail and formatting, but it need not be complex. Its major purpose is to serve as an early warning system for you, particularly on aspects of the application that may take longer than you expect. Completing the chart forces you do to a significant amount of research, in itself enough reason to try this approach. Any other organizational or inspirational benefit it provides is a bonus.

Once your chart is ready, you can begin to focus on each specific element of the application. Every one has its own unique characteristics and time line.

THE PERSONAL STATEMENT

The personal statement causes the most stress of any part of the application (although the LSAT probably wins the overall award for stress creation). After all, this is the one aspect of the application that is neither a historical event nor at the mercy of someone else. As a consequence, law school applicants tend to strive for perfection on the personal statement, over which they have complete control.

The difficulty is, it is not clear what perfection is in this context. The application usually contains a deceptively simple question that provides almost no guidance as to the style and content of your essay. A typical question would be

> The Admissions Committee believes that all relevant factors should be considered when selecting an entering class. You should therefore write a statement describing yourself and your qualifications. You may wish to explain or emphasize a particular part of your transcript or application. You are invited to inform the Committee of achievements and qualities not otherwise revealed by the application.

This query raises more substantive issues than it answers. What are the relevant factors? What part of your application do you want to emphasize? Admissions officers refuse to specify a particular motif or theme they like to see, thus avoiding the inevitable deluge of identical statements that would follow. This also reflects the fact that the admissions officers want to draw a diverse student body. The law schools essentially throw you the ball and then judge the merits of how you throw it back.

In addition, the personal statement causes stress because of its importance in the admissions process. Some admissions personnel consider the personal statement to be the most important part of the application, at least once the minimum GPA/LSAT score has been met. The personal statement is your best chance to speak directly to the reader of your application, to go beyond terse summaries of your accomplishments, and to explain holes in your application. This is quite a bundle of responsibility for a document that is unlikely to be longer than two pages.

Even though not every law school attaches great importance to the personal statement, you should not alter the way you approach the statement. First, you will not know how important the essay is to a given school before you apply. Second, even if it is not that important for most applications at that school, your application may be one of the few where it is. A poor effort could hurt you just as much as a good essay could help. Why take the chance?

How to Ease the Stress of Writing the Personal Statement

First, give yourself enough time to work on the essay. Crafting the statement may take weeks. Inspiration may not come immediately, and this is not an occasion to wait until desperation forces your hand. Furthermore, you want to allow enough time for several other readers to look at your drafts. These readers might be pre-law advisers, faculty, family, or friends. These resources can do more than check for simple mistakes in grammar or spelling; they may also contribute valuable suggestions, topics, or themes you may have overlooked. What do *they* think is the most impressive thing about you? The one disadvantage you must guard against is the tendency for multiple reviewers to edit the life out of an essay, as each person slashes yet another interesting bit.

Most applicants submit essentially the same essay to each school. Admissions personnel do not expect to get an essay that is obviously applicable solely to their school. This does not mean that admissions personnel might not be impressed by the dedication and interest of an applicant who takes the time to tailor the statement to the school. If you want to invest the time to write different statements, make sure that you have specific points about the school to make. A reference to a specific quality of the school, such as a unique clinical program or a reputation for developing public interest lawyers, is more effective than superficial blanket statements declaring your undying love for Prestigious Law School.

The Content of the Personal Statement

The absence of any "correct" approach or content for your personal statement does have one positive aspect: there is virtually no "wrong" approach either. Try to keep this perspective as you contemplate the blank piece of paper. Keep one thought in mind as you ponder. There is a definite value to keeping the statement *interesting*. Readers have to wade through hundreds of earnest declarations of love for their law school. Even the most dedicated officer's eyes glaze over on the hundredth "I want to become a lawyer to improve the world" essay, regardless of its merits, unless the writer can engage the reader's attention.

There are many things that your personal statement could accomplish: it could describe your motivation for going to law school; it could elaborate on a particularly meaningful or impressive accomplishment or event in your life; it could illustrate a unique perspective you would bring to law school; or it could just reflect your thoughts on an issue.

Any of these approaches could be interesting, or any could be dull. You want to describe a facet of yourself that compels a second look. With hindsight Chris now feels that his personal statement was earnest and covered his accomplishments, but its straightforward approach did not make him stand out in any way. He had much better success with an additional essay he wrote for one school, which described student elections he witnessed at his university in India. The latter topic area covered much less of his personal history, but it was much more memorable and provided a forum for commentary on law and democracy in a different context than the norm. He would probably have been better off if he had developed this second essay into his main essay.

Similarly, your first effort or idea is unlikely to be your best one, so do not worry excessively about your first draft. Try to sketch out different ideas over a page or two—personal statements rarely go past two

double-spaced pages—and see which approach holds the most promise. Then sweat over the details and make sure that the statement is written well. Typos and grammatical mistakes on the personal statement look horrendous.

People often use the personal statement to address a specific weakness in their application. For instance, if your GPA is clearly below the standard for the school but you can show that it was low because of one unfortunate year (the first-year immersion problem), an unfortunate choice of classes (the failed pre-med story), or some other unusual outside factor (sickness, work commitment), the personal statement is one chance to make your case to the reader. Exercise restraint on the amount of time and space you give to this apology. There is a limit to the good it will do (it is difficult for a reader to mentally boost someone's LSAT score a few points simply on the basis that the person does not "test well"), and it sets a poor tone. The essay should sing your praises, not draw attention to your flaws. Look for other ways to communicate this kind of negative information. Some law schools allow you to attach pages specifically for these explanations. Consider the option even if they do not; at worst, it will not be read. Your dean's office or academic recommendations may also be forums for others to help you deal with this problem.

You will be the best source of ideas for selling yourself, but look to your friends, family, and advisers to enhance your creativity. Seek out examples of how other people have approached this obstacle from veteran applicants, friends, pre-law advisers, or the books that collect examples of law school essays. Just remember that you should be comfortable with the approach you finally take. It should reflect the kind of person you are and the type of law student you will be.

BIOGRAPHICAL DATA, TRANSCRIPTS, AND SCORES

Completing the biographical information that law schools want causes appreciably less angst than the personal statement. You are constrained to dealing with events that have already occurred, leaving less room for creativity. As a consequence, thoroughness and attention to detail are the demands for these questions.

Clearly, the most important parts of your application are your LSAT score and your undergraduate GPA. Virtually every law school uses a central clearinghouse, the Law School Data Assembly Service (LSDAS), to collect and distribute this information. This simplifies your life somewhat and provides the law schools with a nice tool to compare all their applicants. You, of course, are still responsible for making sure that the LSDAS gets all the relevant material and transcripts and that the right law schools get your report.

Most people subscribe to the LSDAS when they register for the LSAT (see Appendix B for the address of Law Services). The Law Services LSAT registration book will also have the LSDAS forms. You fill in the forms and send in a check (currently $77, although Law Services has a fee waiver program). The fee buys you a one-year membership with the LSDAS, so only subscribe if you plan on applying within the next year. You do not have to make up your mind immediately, as you can sign up later if you change your mind. After you subscribe you must send one official version of all your undergraduate and graduate transcripts to the LSDAS.

The LSDAS collects your biographical information, your transcripts, and your LSAT results to create a Law School Report, which is sent to you and the law schools that you request. The report consists of three elements: all your LSAT scores and writing sample copies, copies of all your transcripts, and an undergraduate academic summary. The last element is where the LSDAS converts your undergraduate grades into a standardized format. The Law School Report provides a cumulative GPA for your entire undergraduate career, a GPA for each year you were in school, and an indicator of where your GPA ranks among everyone else from your school who subscribed to the LSDAS. This allows admissions people to assess your life at a glance while retaining the option of looking more closely at your transcript if they desire. The summary provides a rough class rank (which not all colleges publish) and an easy way to determine trends in your grades (i.e., distinct improvement from your first year to your senior year).

The final step is ensuring that your Law School Report is sent to the right places. You tell the appropriate law schools to request the report from the LSDAS by sending them LSDAS matching forms with your application. Unfortunately, the LSDAS does not do this for free; you have to pay for each report after the first one (somehow this is not included in the initial fee). You do not have to know the number of school reports you need when you subscribe to the LSDAS because you can add as you apply.

The other parts of the biographical sections involve less logistical work. Most of the questions are basic: addresses, educational background, age, and so on. There will usually be some limited space to describe your extracurricular activities, work experience, and honors received. Do not feel constrained by the inadequate space on the forms that the average law school provides to answer these questions, particularly if you have significant work experience. Attach supplementary pages. The limited space is a signal to be succinct, but make sure that any important activity or experience you have had is clearly described. A job title is unlikely to fully communicate the extent of what you did or learned in a particular job.

Think about how your answers to these questions fit with the rest of your application, particularly your personal statement. Are there activities or experiences that substantiate what you expressed in the essay? If there are, make sure they are prominently displayed and fully explained.

LETTERS OF RECOMMENDATION

Law schools often require several letters of recommendation from academic or professional contacts. The letters are meant to give admissions personnel a better sense of the individual behind the application file by gathering outside "objective" opinions. Of course, the writers of these letters are not objective, since they are carefully chosen by the applicant, but most schools play along with the fiction.

The weight schools give to these letters varies. They are definitely secondary to your GPA and LSAT score. The best endorsements in the world will not overcome low scores, but they might make a difference for people on the edge. Consequently, you should take them seriously. Even if the school doesn't demand letters, send some. Do not be afraid to send more letters than required unless the school explicitly limits the number.

The decision about whom to ask for a recommendation can be daunting. The one universal piece of advice that admissions officers give about these testimonials is that the recommender should know you well. The common fallacy is that admissions personnel will be most impressed with an endorsement from an important legal person, such as a dean or judge. This is only true if the person can say something coherent about you as an individual. A short paragraph full of generalities from a Supreme Court Justice who knows your Aunt Elizabeth will interest an admissions officer much less than a page of praise from a junior faculty member who can back up the compliments with specific examples and comparisons to other students. Admissions officers may even be insulted by your underestimation of their sophistication.

You want to have at least one academic recommendation. Faculty members are in a good position to assess the intellectual abilities that law schools most desire. Assess the relationships you have developed with the faculty at your college or in graduate school. Again, the fame of the evaluator will be less important than the closeness of the relationship. Ideally, you have several professors who know you well enough to write glowing and individualized recommendations. If you do not have these connections, work to create them. Try to take a seminar or a small class. Failing that, go to office hours of one of your current or former professors. Invest the time and effort in making yourself known so the teacher can say more than, "Rachel wrote a good term paper and got an A in my class."

Admissions officers are aware that getting a good academic recommendation becomes more difficult the longer you are out of an academic environment. It is acceptable to substitute a professional contact for the academic one if you have serious difficulties finding an academic source. Attaching a brief note explaining why you had a problem getting an academic recommendation is a good idea.

Use all your diplomatic skills when you request recommendations. You are, after all, asking for the time of a busy person. Make sure that you give advance warning and enough time for the person to write at their convenience. You should be particularly vigilant about making sure that your letters of recommendation are completed and sent out on time, since absent-minded or busy professors are notoriously poor with deadlines. Exert as much pressure as you tactfully can. Observe the formal niceties of thank you letters, and ease the logistical hassles as much as possible.

Your diplomatic skills may be useful in a second context as well. Ideally, you will work with your recommender to shape what he or she writes so that it is both a good evaluation and complements the rest of your application. This does not require that you actually write the testimonial yourself (although this does happen); there are less blatant interventions. Tell your writers the themes you hope to communicate in your application. Give them copies of your resume, transcript, and anything else that gives them a better picture of you. Many recommenders will be quite open to suggestion. Remember, they are on your side.

Many schools also require an evaluation from the dean's office. The form will ask what, if any, disciplinary or academic problems you had at college. Don't worry if your Dean of Students couldn't pick you out of a lineup; few people have a close relationship with their dean. The form primarily serves as a check to make sure there is no dirty laundry that an applicant might not disclose voluntarily. A few colleges try to give their graduates an edge by ensuring that the dean's letter also serves as a real recommendation, but this is the exception. Take advantage of any such system if it exists, but otherwise expect little benefit from this element. If there is something uncomplimentary in your record that will show up in the dean's letter make sure that your side of the story is laid out in your application.

LAW SCHOOL INTERVIEWS

Notably absent from this chapter thus far is mention of an interview. Few law schools use evaluative interviews in their admissions process. Most schools encourage potential candidates to visit the school and will set up activities, interviews, or otherwise cater to interested parties, but rarely will these interactions reach your application file. There are other excellent reasons to visit law schools (see Chapter 10), so you should still visit despite the minimal effect on your admissions chances.

There are a few law schools that use an interview at some point, although sometimes only for borderline candidates. More schools simply encourage interviews if they are possible. If a law school does use an interview at some stage in its process, definitely take advantage of the opportunity if you can. You should seize any chance you have to add depth and life to your application. If you have an interview, make sure you have done your research about the school, have some intelligent questions (even if you already know the answers, ask intelligent questions), and be prepared to talk about anything that appeared on your application. This is another chance to emphasize the core themes you developed in your application.

FINANCIAL AID APPLICATIONS

As we discussed in Chapter 12, financial aid in some form is a prerequisite for attending law school for almost everyone. Law schools are aware of this and do their best to make it possible for students to get the financial help they need. After all, it makes perfect sense for the law schools to share your concern about your ability to pay your tuition bills. The positive consequence of this shared interest is that financial aid offices can be a useful resource for help and advice on battling through the forms and red tape. You should jump through all the financial aid hoops if there is even a remote possibility that you will need assistance. This precaution can save you money and hassle.

You should approach your financial aid application with the same rigor and care as you do the rest of your application. The paperwork in this area is worse than in any other part of the application process, so your primary worry will be tracking it. Remember that on loan matters you will deal with the financial aid office of the law school or university, not the admissions people; do not cross your correspondence streams. You must keep a careful eye on the clerical requirements and the deadlines that accompany different sources of assistance. Use a tracking chart of due dates and assignments for yourself so you know what has to be done when. Keep copies of everything, file forms on time, and otherwise take care of the nitpicky details (this is good practice for a lawyer).

The other major piece of advice is that, just as with the application itself, you should apply for financial aid early. There are several reasons for this. The most important one is that law schools have finite amounts of financial aid. As they commit their money, the pot dwindles for the last people in line. Delay may mean that you do not get all the aid you might have if you had been first in line. In addition, the faster you complete the forms, the faster the schools can make the aid decisions that are likely to influence your choice of schools. The definition of *early* in financial aid terms depends on the school, since each has a different process. Generally, since applications require your or your parents' tax returns, the earliest you can apply is in January (this may require you to file your tax returns early).

There are other things you can do to prepare yourself. If you do not already, budget your expenditures for a few months. This snapshot of your standard of living will help you understand the consequences of different assistance packages you might receive. Check on your credit rating as well. You can do this for free or for a nominal fee by calling a credit agency and requesting your credit report. A poor credit history will hamper your quest to get loans from anyone, so make sure that there are no mistakes on the report (an all too common phenomenon). This applies even to those who do not have credit cards, since things as petty as a missed gas bill can show up and lower your credit rating. It is critical that you not be in default on a government loan or grant refund, since this will prevent you from applying for federal financial aid successfully. If you are in default, contact the loan agency and the school to learn how to change your status.

Eventually, all your application materials will be in the mail. Now you can relax for a while. Check your mail for notices that your application file is complete (if the school sends them out), and call the school if nothing appears. Otherwise, relax, fulfill whatever rituals bring you good luck, and wait.

15

THE ENDGAME

The tests are taken, the forms are filled, and the applications are mailed. There is little to do while you sit back and wait for the big, bulky envelopes to fill your mailbox (just as with college rejections, the thin envelope is the harbinger of doom). Enjoy this eye of the storm, as there may be a few major decisions on the horizon.

WHEN WILL YOU HEAR?

This phase in the application cycle represents a reversal of roles. You can relax (relatively, as you may find that the burdens of the nonapplication part of your world have piled up during the process) while the law schools have to scramble frenetically to process, review, and decide on everyone's application. Law schools try to make their decisions as expeditiously as they can, since earlier responses reduce tension for candidates and increase the odds that they get the people they want, but this process takes time, particularly given the number of applicants. The response time for law schools ranges from a few weeks to a few months from when they get your materials. As a general rule, law schools sort out their class and respond during March, April, and May, but there sometimes are significant deviations from this timing.

You can make an estimate of the earliest date you could get a response. The law schools provide a rough guideline of when they begin to respond. Undergraduates also hear through the grapevine about the success or failure of their classmates. In any case, the actual time it will take depends on two elements:

- the institutional method of evaluating applications
- the strength of your application compared to the rest of the applicant pool

The first element is the more important. Every school needs at least a few weeks to request, receive, and review your LSDAS report, so this is the bare minimum. Schools that depend heavily upon the easily quantifiable scores, such as your LSAT score and GPA, can make their decisions quickly after they process the paperwork. Schools that pay more attention to the subjective elements of the application, such as letters of recommendation or the personal statement, take longer. Institutions that want to see the whole pool of applicants before making decisions are not going to be able to respond until a long period after their filing deadline, while schools that practice rolling admissions can make their decision as soon as they receive your complete file.

The second element is the strength of your application. Clearly superior or inferior applications can be dealt with quickly. Tougher calls must wait longer. Admissions officers do not want to make a premature decision on a borderline applicant, so they push back the ultimate decision. Even schools that practice rolling admissions preserve the option of deferring the decision about a particular person until they have seen the entire pool. Under this scenario, a delay in receiving a response might mean that you could be in the final cut, but it also means you will not get a definite answer until the end of the acceptance period for that school. Many schools try to reduce anxiety by letting applicants know if they have deferred their decision. This helps to a degree. Deferral at least proves that you have not been rejected, but of course it also means that you have not yet been accepted either. Deferral is one of those half-full, half-empty types of responses.

Anxiety is natural once you recognize that your law schools have begun to send out responses. The trip to the mailbox becomes a tension-filled ritual. Stories and rumors about successful and unsuccessful fellow applicants simply aggravate this stress. Unfortunately, there is little you can do to ease this tension. Admissions offices discourage repeated phone calls to check on your status. They will contact you as soon as they can. Remember that many slots are not filled immediately, and do not give up hope until you actually receive a rejection letter.

WHAT IF THE ANSWER IS YES?

The tell-tale sign of acceptance is the thick envelope full of propaganda, financial aid information, and, yes, a page of congratulations and welcome to the hallowed halls of Law School X. You may become one of the anointed few. The slender envelope, on the other hand, spells doom or, at best, delay.

As the results come back, you have to decide where to accept. The difficulty of the decision after you get your replies will depend heavily on the number of fat envelopes you receive, but it is rarely a clear-cut choice. One common "problem" people face is when they have offers from roughly comparable schools. The difficulty of choosing one law school from among several suitors may not get you much sympathy, but it can cause serious angst.

Your approach to deciding between your offers should parallel the sorting process you made when you first applied. Build on the research you have already done. It is easier to motivate yourself to research at this stage because this is no longer a theoretical exercise. The approach laid out in Chapters 10, 11, and 12 will work here as well, with the obvious exception that you do not have to worry about your chances of admission anymore. "All" you have to do is figure out which school is best for you, given its cost.

The balance of power has shifted in your favor. Now that you are in the enviable position of choosing between law schools, the admissions staff must sell you on the merits of their school. Law schools use a combination of letters, phone calls, propaganda, and arranged tours of the campus to woo their prospective students. Admissions staff will generally bend over backwards to accommodate requests for information or contacts.

If you applied for financial aid early enough, you will also have the advantage of comparing financial aid packages. Law schools try to determine aid awards as soon as possible, particularly those that are not need-based, so you will generally be able to make an informed assessment of how much your education will cost you. Remember that the law schools are now bidding for you. Let the admissions staff know about generous offers of financial assistance you may get from their rivals. You may be able to use these offers as leverage to get a better package from the school you think would be best for you.

Law schools are generally good about allowing you enough time to make an informed decision. You do not have to make decisions immediately or keep only one offer open at a time. The law schools will ask for a response by a certain date in the acceptance letter. As a general rule, the later you hear from the law school, the less time you will have to respond. The Law School Admission Council policy states that law schools should permit applicants to choose among offers with no penalty until April 1. After this point, many, but not all, law schools will require a deposit to preserve an offer of acceptance. The deposits typically run in the hundreds of dollars and are eventually applied as a credit against your tuition for the first semester. You are still free to accept an offer from another law school after you put down the deposit, but you will probably forfeit all or part of the money. This does put pressure on people who are still waiting to hear from one place after the deposit deadline of another. Part of this pressure is by design, but if you are in that position, you should explain your situation to the admissions staff of the institution that wants the deposit. They can accommodate exceptional cases, and you really have nothing to lose by trying.

Your choice of a law school is particularly important because it is hard to rectify a mistake. It is possible to transfer from one law school to another, but it is not easy, particularly if you hope to move to a more prestigious place. There are not many openings at most institutions, so do not take a slot at a safety school only because you are sure you will transfer out. It is likely that you will have to stay there.

WHAT IF THE ANSWER IS NO?

If you are not accepted at any of your target schools, do not despair. Many people who have subsequently gone on to law school have shared this fate. The lack of success should make you reassess your approach to the application process. You can try to ask admissions officers of your schools why you were not successful, although many admissions personnel do not like to discuss this topic. If this fails, ask yourself some questions. Did you give your best effort on every element of the application? Did your LSAT score reflect your expectations? Did you include a true safety school among your target schools? You may be able to correct these errors, particularly if you readjust your target pool to encompass some lower-ranked institutions. If you applied early in the cycle, there still may be schools that will accept applications for the next year's class. Otherwise, you have a year to make yourself a better candidate for the next attempt. Many schools make it easy for you to reapply by allowing you to update your old file with a new personal statement and, of course, a new application fee.

ALTERNATIVES TO YES OR NO—
THE WAIT LIST

There is another possible response other than outright rejection or acceptance: the wait list. This option lets the law school sit on the fence, postponing the final decision even further. The school will send you a short note asking you if you are willing to be placed on the wait list. If you are, the school will continue to consider your application until the day classes begin. If a slot opens up, the dean of admissions will work through the names on the wait list until the class is filled.

The use of wait lists reflects the uncertainty shared by the law schools in the whole admissions process. While admissions personnel know how many offers they extended for a given class, they do not know how many bodies will actually show up to register in the fall. There is always some movement in and out of the class until the final days of the summer by people who change their minds about their plans, the program, or law school altogether.

What to Do if You Are on a Wait List

Being on a wait list is form of purgatory that beats total rejection, but not by much. Law schools may put hundreds of people on their wait lists, the vast majority of whom have virtually no chance of entering the sacred halls. The number of people accepted this way, if there are any at all, varies each year. You do not know if you are the first candidate on the list or the last one. Being on the wait list gives a desperate sense of hope that is rarely fulfilled. Furthermore, late acceptances can play havoc with living arrangements, logistics, and deposits. Since many people still jump at the chance to join the select few, the schools get away with the practice.

Chris ended up on several wait lists. This development definitely made his summer more stressful because he had to make several contingency plans, but he eventually did get admitted from a wait list in August, giving him just enough time to plan the beginning of his law school career. It is hard to fight the feeling of helplessness over your fate, even though this is characteristic of much of the law school application process.

One of Harry's law school classmates actually began classes at another school and then finally received a last-minute acceptance off the wait list (Harry's school began classes a week or so later). Harry's friend had to suddenly pull up stakes and move to a new state in a matter of days. The whole process was extremely stressful and jarring, but she wound up at the school she wanted.

The best thing to do if you end up on a wait list is to recognize that this is a long shot. Talk to the admissions staff to get as much information as they will give you. They are likely to know how many people have been taken in past years off the list and should be able to tell you how many people are on the list. Different schools have different policies on how much information they give to individuals on the wait list, but you should at least try to garner as much hard information as you can.

The one thing you can do to improve your chances is to show your continued interest in the school. The qualifications of the people on the list are very close, so enthusiasm is one way make yourself stand out from the pack. Develop your application further, showing your dedication and desire, by sending in your latest transcript, another recommendation, or a letter. Visit the admissions personnel if you can, so that they can attach a face and personality to a name, but use some restraint: you do not want to annoy the admissions staff with daily phone calls.

Conditional Acceptance

Provisional or conditional acceptance programs are another way law schools stay on the fence. Approximately a dozen schools maintain these programs for students who do not meet their normal entrance criteria but who show potential. These candidates are given the option of paying to take law classes at the school in the summer. Those who meet grade cut-offs are then accepted for the entering class in the fall. Those who don't make the grade lose their time and money. This is not an easy way into law school, since the programs are designed to aggressively screen out candidates, so this is usually a last resort for an applicant.

DEFERRING LAW SCHOOL

You may also have a way to keep the law school on the fence. Many schools will let you wait to take advantage of the school's offer of admission until the following academic year if you can show that you would use the time away from academia productively. The law schools that allow you to defer are often quite lenient about what constitutes a productive use of your time. Virtually any significant job or activity is likely to be acceptable. Deferring is a superb deal, as it gives you the luxury of time to do whatever you wish with the security of a spot in the following year's class. All you have to do in exchange is agree that you will not apply to any other school in the intervening year. Law schools generally give you a one-year reprieve, but you may be able to negotiate for additional time after the year is up. Talk to the admissions office; they want their students to have done interesting things, so they are generally sympathetic to plans that may take longer. Do *not* ask these questions before you have been accepted. There is no point in raising questions about your desire to attend the school prior to the admissions decision.

As we stressed in Chapter 9, taking time away from the academic environment before law school is a thoroughly good idea. A deferral year is an ideal time to make sure that law school is really the path you want to take. You may realize that you really want to be cutting cadavers in medical school, not buried in a law library. If law school still appeals to you at the end of the year, you have lost nothing and gained experience. There is so much you can do in a year that will help you to enjoy and succeed in the law school environment that you should at least consider what you could do with your time. This is a unique window of opportunity that you simply will not get again once you begin law school. Use it.

THE LAST SUMMER

When you make your decision and commit to one law school, you finally get to take a break from the application process. Congratulate yourself and devote your time to enjoying your final moments before you start to walk, talk, and breathe the law. The only law school-related work you should do is to figure out your living arrangements for the coming year. You do not want to have to deal with balky landlords during your first weeks of class. Otherwise, relax. Take a vacation. Travel. Do *not* try to get a head start on your classmates by devouring legal treatises or case books during the summer. You will be totally immersed in the law soon enough; enjoy the time you have outside of that environment.

Some will be unable to avoid thinking about the upcoming adventure and may rent old films such as *The Paper Chase* or check out books such as *One L* in order to get in the mood for the first year of law school. Chances are, your experiences will be quite different from those versions, and focusing on them will only increase your pre-school anxiety. Still, there is no denying that whatever your law school years are like, the start of first year will mark a defining moment in your life, dividing all that came before and comes after. After struggling over all the preparation discussed in this book, you may find it hard to believe but the *real* challenge is just about to begin.

SOME LAST WORDS

Throughout this book we have tried to guide you through the entire law school application process, from first inklings to first year. We have exhausted the advice we can give, and now it is up to you to make it happen. The information in this book may confirm for some that they are ready to apply to law school immediately and help others decide that there is no way they would ever subject themselves to such a fate. Depending on your own personality, either choice may be right for you.

The central point of this book is to help you think about all the different issues you face on the road to law school and practicing law. The decision about going to law school is not easy for anyone. You cannot be certain you made the correct choice until you try it. Even then, the challenges that confront you in law school and after you start practicing law ensure that you will revisit that decision throughout your life. The legal profession is the right choice for people who find its combination of intellectual challenges, material rewards, and opportunities to help others extremely satisfying, but it is not for everyone. In the final analysis, law is a reasonable career choice for many, and a great choice for some. In the face of this uncertainty, the best you can do is to focus carefully on what you think is right for you at every stage. Good luck.

APPENDIX A
OTHER HELPFUL BOOKS

There are many books that can provide additional information you will find helpful during your process of applying to law school. Here is a partial listing, with brief notes about each book's highlights.

ARCO—The Best Law Schools, by Thomas H. Martinson (Prentice-Hall, 1993).
Discusses the author's choice of the top 25 law schools in the United States and his 15 runners-up. You can probably guess most of the top 25 already. For the money, you might as well get one of the bigger guides that list more schools.

ARCO—LSAT: Law School Admission Test, by Thomas H. Martinson (Macmillan, 1995).
Just examples of LSAT tests and answers, without much real guidance.

Barron's Guide to Law Schools (Barron's Educational Series, 1994).
This gives information on individual law schools. Contains a nice model LSAT test.

Barron's How to Prepare for the LSAT, by Jerry Bobrow (Barron's Educational Series, 1996).
After a very brief introduction, this thick book is all LSAT test examples.

The Best Test Preparation for the LSAT (Research & Education Association, 1995).
Six complete practice LSAT exams. Very dry.

The Complete Law School Companion, by Jeff Deaver (John Wiley & Sons, 1992).
A nice guide to going to law school. Applying for law school is covered briefly, with the primary focus on how to do well during law school. Al-

most too detailed in discussing tips for succeeding in courses and exams.

Essays That Worked for Law School: 35 Essays from Successful Applications to The Nation's Top Schools, ed. by Boykin Curry (Fawcett Columbine, 1988).

An extremely narrowly focused book, this reprints personal essays from people who were accepted to law school. A nice enough effort, but you're probably better off coming up with your own ideas.

How to Get into Harvard Law School, by Willie J. Epps (Contemporary Books, 1996).

The title calls out for a smart-aleck response (such as "Have dear old dad make a huge contribution to his alma mater") that is probably not warranted. If Harvard, and only Harvard, is what you want, then this is the book for you. Think about broadening your horizons. Maybe think about Yale as your backup school.

How to Get into the Right Law School, by Paul Lermack (VGM Career Horizons, 1996).

Well-written though somewhat dense writing style. This book assumes you have pretty much already decided to go to law school.

How to Succeed in Law School, by Gary A. Munneke (Barron's Educational Series, 1994).

Well-organized walk-through of the law school experience. Highlights are the numerous reprints from actual law school course books that give a real taste of what law school reading is all about.

Looking at Law School: A Student Guide from the Society of Law School Teachers, ed. by Stephen Gillers (Meridian, 1990).

A collection of sometimes rambling essays on the general topic of law school by various professors. The focus is on being *in* law school, not thinking about *going* to law school. Supreme Court Justice William J. Brennan writes an introduction.

The Official Guide to U.S. Law Schools, by the Law School Admission Council (Bantam Doubleday Dell, 1996).

Defense and Education Fund
14th floor
3

The standard reference on the topic. This contains some of the same discussions included in *So You Want to Be a Lawyer* (see below) but adds voluminous information on individual law schools.

The Princeton Review: Cracking the LSAT (Random House, 1996).
Glitzy, short, and with big print. Implies you'll learn some sort of "secret" to "crack" the confidential code behind the LSAT. Right . . .

The Princeton Review Law School Companion, by Paul M. Lisnek and Steven I. Friedland (Princeton Review, 1995).
Focuses on the process of *going* to law school, without saying much about *applying* for law school.

The Princeton Review Student Access Guide to the Best Law Schools, by Ian Van Tuyl (Random House, 1996).
A more "human" touch to the same idea as *The Official Guide to U.S. Law Schools* (see above). After a somewhat superfluous discussion of the history of U.S. law schools, the book moves on to a nicely organized listing of U.S. law schools. Each school is concisely summarized at the top of its page. There is also a useful series of bar charts for each school, for topics such as employment breakdown of alumnae.

REA's Authoritative Guide to Law Schools (Research & Education Association, 1994).
Begins with a brief overview of the general issues involved in going to law school and then focuses on school-by-school information, including lots of statistics.

Slaying the Law School Dragon, by George Roth (John Wiley & Sons, 1991).
Somewhat turgid, this book jumps all over the place to cover several topics dealing with the first year of law school.

So You Want to Be a Lawyer: A Practical Guide to Law as a Career, by the Law School Admission Council (Bantam Doubleday Dell, 1996).
A nice summary of the entire topic, but it suffers from being an "official" publication from the producers of the LSAT (it is somewhat dry and reserved). Oddly, it only spends four pages discussing the LSAT! It contains a nice geographic list of law schools.

Puerto Rican Lega
99 Hudson Street—
New York, NY 100
212-219-3360

Information o

Law Services
Box 2000
661 Penn Stre
Newtown, PA
LSDAS auton

Information

Department c
1-800-433-3

Information

Law School
Law Service
Box 40
Newtown, P
215-968-11

Informatio

Council on
1420 N Str
Washingtor
202-785-4

Mexican-A
634 South
Los Angel
213-629-2

APPENDIX C
SAMPLE LAW SCHOOL APPLICATION TIME LINE

This sample is designed to provide only a basic overview of the typical timing of events during the process of applying to law school. You should make your own schedule based upon the application due dates for your target law schools. Remember, it is to your advantage to finish each stage of the application process early.

August/September
Research and select your target schools.
Send for applications.
Make application schedule for your target schools.
Register for the LSAT October test.
Subscribe to the LSDAS.
Arrange for your transcripts to be sent to LSDAS.
Study for the LSAT.

October
Take October LSAT.
Arrange for letters of recommendation.

November
Complete applications.
Receive LSAT scores.

December
Mail applications.
Take December LSAT (if necessary).

January/February
Federal financial aid applications become available.
Complete financial aid applications.

March/April/May
Receive responses from law schools.
Visit schools.
Receive financial aid determinations from law schools.
Make decisions and submit admissions deposit.

June/July
Relax.

August/September
Register and begin law school.

The standard reference on the topic. This contains some of the same discussions included in *So You Want to Be a Lawyer* (see below) but adds voluminous information on individual law schools.

The Princeton Review: Cracking the LSAT (Random House, 1996).
Glitzy, short, and with big print. Implies you'll learn some sort of "secret" to "crack" the confidential code behind the LSAT. Right . . .

The Princeton Review Law School Companion, by Paul M. Lisnek and Steven I. Friedland (Princeton Review, 1995).
Focuses on the process of *going* to law school, without saying much about *applying* for law school.

The Princeton Review Student Access Guide to the Best Law Schools, by Ian Van Tuyl (Random House, 1996).
A more "human" touch to the same idea as *The Official Guide to U.S. Law Schools* (see above). After a somewhat superfluous discussion of the history of U.S. law schools, the book moves on to a nicely organized listing of U.S. law schools. Each school is concisely summarized at the top of its page. There is also a useful series of bar charts for each school, for topics such as employment breakdown of alumnae.

REA's Authoritative Guide to Law Schools (Research & Education Association, 1994).
Begins with a brief overview of the general issues involved in going to law school and then focuses on school-by-school information, including lots of statistics.

Slaying the Law School Dragon, by George Roth (John Wiley & Sons, 1991).
Somewhat turgid, this book jumps all over the place to cover several topics dealing with the first year of law school.

So You Want to Be a Lawyer: A Practical Guide to Law as a Career, by the Law School Admission Council (Bantam Doubleday Dell, 1996).
A nice summary of the entire topic, but it suffers from being an "official" publication from the producers of the LSAT (it is somewhat dry and reserved). Oddly, it only spends four pages discussing the LSAT! It contains a nice geographic list of law schools.

APPENDIX B
SOURCES OF INFORMATION

Information on the LSAT and LSDAS

Law Services
Box 2000
661 Penn Street
Newtown, PA 18940-0988
LSDAS automated information number: 215-968-1300

Information on Federal Student Loans and the FAFSA

Department of Education
1-800-433-3243

Information on Law School Fairs

Law School Forums
Law Services
Box 40
Newtown, PA 18940-0040
215-968-1120

Information on Minority Scholarship Opportunities

Council on Legal Education Opportunity
1420 N Street NW #T-1
Washington, D.C. 20005
202-785-4840

Mexican-American Legal Defense and Educational Fund
634 South Spring Street—11th floor
Los Angeles, CA 90014
213-629-2512

Puerto Rican Legal Defense and Education Fund
99 Hudson Street—14th floor
New York, NY 10013
212-219-3360

APPENDIX C
SAMPLE LAW SCHOOL APPLICATION TIME LINE

This sample is designed to provide only a basic overview of the typical timing of events during the process of applying to law school. You should make your own schedule based upon the application due dates for your target law schools. Remember, it is to your advantage to finish each stage of the application process early.

August/September
Research and select your target schools.
Send for applications.
Make application schedule for your target schools.
Register for the LSAT October test.
Subscribe to the LSDAS.
Arrange for your transcripts to be sent to LSDAS.
Study for the LSAT.

October
Take October LSAT.
Arrange for letters of recommendation.

November
Complete applications.
Receive LSAT scores.

December
Mail applications.
Take December LSAT (if necessary).

January/February
Federal financial aid applications become available.
Complete financial aid applications.

March/April/May
Receive responses from law schools.
Visit schools.
Receive financial aid determinations from law schools.
Make decisions and submit admissions deposit.

June/July
Relax.

August/September
Register and begin law school.

INDEX

199

ABOUT THE AUTHORS

Harry Castleman has been practicing law since 1982 and is currently senior business counsel with the law firm of Gaffin & Krattenmaker, P.C., in Boston, Massachusetts, specializing in corporate work and trusts and estates. He is a member of both the Massachusetts and Florida bars. A graduate of Northwestern University in Evanston, Illinois, and a cum laude graduate of Boston University Law School, he has co-authored eight books on popular culture, ranging from the history of television to the Beatles. Before going to law school, he worked for the Democratic National Committee in Washington, D.C., and the Florida Democratic Party as well as in several statewide petition campaigns of Florida Governor Reubin Askew. Harry is happily married and is the father of a very cute and very smart young lady. Just ask him.

Christopher Niewoehner is a graduate of Harvard College and Harvard Law School. While attending law school, he served as a pre-law adviser to Harvard undergraduates. He worked in Washington, D.C., for the Department of Health and Human Services and traveled to India for a year prior to entering law school. He plans to clerk for a judge in Chicago and then explore the range of possibilities of a law degree.